# How to Pass

SECOND EDITION

## HIGHER

# French

Douglas Angus

HODDER
GIBSON

AN HACHETTE UK COMPANY

**Audio files for the Listening tasks in this book are available online. Visit www.hoddergibson.co.uk and click on 'Updates and Extras'.**

The Publishers would like to thank the following for permission to reproduce copyright material.

### Acknowledgements

The reading passage 'Le Français en vacances : ce qui a changé' (pp.3–4), questions (pp.4–7) and marking scheme (p.8); the contexts and topics grid in Appendix 1 (p.115); the talking and writing grammar guide in Appendix 2 (p.116); and the marking scheme tables in Appendices 3 and 4 (pp.117–23) copyright © Scottish Qualifications Authority.

The solutions to worked examples throughout the book are by the author.

The reading passage 'La mode du sport : les baskets et les jogging !' (pp.20–1) is based on the article 'Va y avoir du style' by Françoise-Marie Santucci, which appeared in *Libération* on 16 June 2006; permission granted by EDD.

Reading passage (pp.14–15) is adapted from 'La vogue des rencontres sur Internet' published on DossierFamilial.com 5 September 2007; reading passage (pp.17–18) based on 'Scolarité : le redoublement est-il un échec ?' also from DossierFamilial.com, published on 12 May 2014; reading passage (pp.23–4) is adapted from 'SMS, textos : dites Je t'M avec le pouce !' by Louis Asana published on Doctissimo.com.

Audio engineering: Phil Booth, Heriot-Watt University, Edinburgh.

Every effort has been made to trace all copyright holders, but if any have been inadvertently overlooked, the Publishers will be pleased to make the necessary arrangements at the first opportunity.

Although every effort has been made to ensure that website addresses are correct at time of going to press, Hodder Gibson cannot be held responsible for the content of any website mentioned in this book. It is sometimes possible to find a relocated web page by typing in the address of the home page for a website in the URL window of your browser.

Hachette UK's policy is to use papers that are natural, renewable and recyclable products and made from wood grown in well-managed forests and other controlled sources. The logging and manufacturing processes are expected to conform to the environmental regulations of the country of origin.

Orders: please contact Bookpoint Ltd, 130 Park Drive, Milton Park, Abingdon, Oxon OX14 4SE. Telephone: (44) 01235 827827. Fax: (44) 01235 400454. Email education@bookpoint.co.uk. Lines are open from 9 a.m. to 5 p.m., Monday to Saturday, with a 24-hour message answering service. Visit our website at www.hoddereducation.co.uk. Hodder Gibson can also be contacted directly at hoddergibson@hodder.co.uk

Cover photo © Zarya Maxim - stock.adobe.com
Illustrations by Barking Dog Art Design and Illustrations
Typeset in 13/15 Cronos Pro (Light) by Aptara, Inc
Printed in India
A catalogue record for this title is available from the British Library.
ISBN: 978 1 5104 5246 6

# Contents

# Introduction

Welcome to *How to Pass Higher French*! Higher French assesses your skills in French through four skill areas, and this book will show you how to get the best possible mark in each area. There are separate sections giving advice on reading, listening, talking and writing. For reading and listening, there are also practice questions, with answers so that you can check your work. For talking and writing, we work through some sample questions, looking at how to improve your performance in assessments. Accompanying this book are soundfiles that can be downloaded from www.hoddergibson.co.uk (click on 'Updates and Extras'), and in the book there are questions and transcripts to go with these soundfiles.

# What is involved in Higher French?

Higher French, like National 5, is a course that is tested by assessments carried out in class, and also in an external exam. In class with your teacher, you will produce evidence for talking and writing. You will be involved in deciding what the subjects of these two assessments will be. The external exam at the end of the course will be set and marked by SQA, and will test your reading, listening and writing skills. What is new in the external exam at Higher, as opposed to National 5, is translation: you will be asked to translate a short extract of the reading passage from French into English.

# How is my final mark made up?

All your marks for the four parts of the exam are added together to make your final mark, which is out of 120. However, as each of the four skills is worth 30 marks, or **25%** of your final mark, the individual marks will be 'scaled', that is, converted to a mark which allows equal weighting for all four skills. This happened at National 5 as well. As you work your way through this book, the individual weightings will be explained. Remember, you can fail an individual part of the exam, but still pass overall. Normally, 70% is an A, 60% is a B, 50% a C and 45% will get a D.

## Talking

This is marked out of 30 (which is **25%** of your overall mark). You will start off with a general conversation, before moving on to the topics you have chosen to talk about. The assessment should last about 10 minutes. You can find more about this in the chapter on talking (Chapter 9).

## Reading and translation

This makes up **25%** of your mark. 20 marks are given for the answers to the questions on the passage and 10 marks for the translation. That makes a total of 30 marks.

# Directed writing

You will be asked to write an account, in French, of a visit you have made to, or an experience you have had in, a French-speaking country. (You do not actually have to have made this visit as it can be imaginary.) There will be a choice of two topics, taken from two of the four contexts: Society, Learning, Employability and Culture. You will be asked to address six specific bullet points. This will be marked out of 20, and then scaled to a mark of 15 to be worth **12.5%** of your overall mark.

# Listening

This makes up **25%** of your overall mark. It is marked out of 20, and then scaled to a mark out of 30. You will hear a presentation or monologue, followed by a dialogue. The topic will be taken from one of the four contexts: Society, Learning, Employability and Culture.

# Assignment-writing

You will be asked to write, in class, about a topic you have chosen with your teacher, discussing it, giving your opinions and coming to a conclusion. This writing will be marked out of 20, but, like the directed writing, is worth **12.5%** of your overall mark.

# What do I have to know?

You will be expected to know all the basic vocabulary of French, but also vocabulary covering a list of the contexts and topic areas of Higher, which are in the Structures and vocabulary chapter (Chapter 12). This will help you listen to and read French more easily. In this book we have reprinted basic vocabulary to help you revise, and have added to this useful vocabulary for each of the four contexts of Higher.

You will also need to know more about grammar than you did at National 5, so that you can write and speak French at the appropriate level for Higher. Your writing should show you have some knowledge of grammar, and you must work at getting your structures and endings right. The grammar guide in the chapter on Structures and vocabulary (Chapter 12) should give you an idea of what you are expected to know. In talking, your teacher and examiner will be looking for you to demonstrate a knowledge of structure, verbs and the other aspects of language that are in the grammar guide.

You must also be able to use a good dictionary to help you understand French in the reading exam, and to let you find words you need for your talking and writing. This means you need to know properly how your dictionary works, how to look up words quickly and how to interpret what you find when you have looked something up. You will find some advice on this in the reading chapter of this book (Chapter 1).

# What exactly is involved in the exam?

There are three parts to the exam: the first two will often take place in February and March and will be your talking assessment and your writing assignment. The second part comprises Papers 1 and 2, which you will sit in May. Paper 1 lasts two hours, and is made up of Reading, Translation and Directed writing. Paper 2 is Listening and will last for 30 minutes.

## Talking

Talking will be assessed by your teacher and may be externally moderated by SQA. What you talk about should be organised between you and your teacher.

You will have to carry out two tasks:
- An initial informal conversation with your teacher to help you settle into the task, then
- a discussion with your teacher, starting on one of the topics you have chosen. You must move on to another topic area during the course of the conversation. This should last about ten minutes. You are allowed some written support notes, using no more than five headings of up to eight words each in English or in French.

Remember, it is a conversation, so you can lead it where you want it to go and decide when to move on from one topic to another. There is more advice on this in Chapter 9 (Talking).

## Listening

For the Course, listening will be assessed by the external Higher exam. This will be a recording of a monologue by one French speaker, followed by a dialogue between two French speakers, and you will be asked to give answers based upon what you hear. The monologue will last up to two minutes, and the dialogue will last over two minutes. You will hear them both twice (not three times as at National 5 level). There will be a gap between the monologue and the dialogue, and you will be warned when there is a minute to go till the start of the dialogue.

The questions will be set and answered in English, and will follow the order of the dialogue.

## Reading and translation

The Course Reading paper is one longer text, of about 600 words, with questions that will be set and answered in English. You may well find unusual words translated for you in a glossary. You will be allowed to use a French/English dictionary, and will have to be good at using this, as otherwise you will spend so much time looking up words, you will never finish answering the questions!

One part of the reading text will be underlined (usually a small paragraph, or three to four sentences) and you will be asked to translate this into English.

Most of the questions will follow the order of the text, and you will be guided as to where to find the answers. However, one question will ask you to identify the overall purpose or meaning of the text.

## Writing

Writing will be assessed in two ways. You will have to produce two pieces of writing:

- **Directed writing** of 150 to 180 words, which will be an account of a journey or experience you have made, chosen from two options. There will be six bullet points to address, which you should attempt to answer at roughly equal length.
- **Assignment-writing** of 200 to 250 words, which will be linked to a topic you have chosen. There will be an overall question in English as part of the task to address, and a couple of questions (also in English) to help guide your answer.

For both of these pieces of writing you will be allowed a dictionary.

# What grammar do I need to know?

When marking your work, teachers will be looking for a variety of different structures, a good level of accuracy in basic structures and some control of more complex language. You will be allowed to make some errors, but this will affect the grade you are awarded. You should be able to show you can do everything listed in the box below.

For better grades, you will have to do more than this. Marking schemes show what examiners are going to be looking for, and the marking schemes and grade descriptors for Talking and Writing, which you will find in Appendix 3 and Appendix 4, will give you a clear idea of what you should be able to do to achieve a good mark.

## What you should know 👍

### Verbs

- ★ Use the correct form of the present, imperfect, perfect, future and conditional tenses, and use modal verbs correctly.
- ★ Use *ne ... pas, ne ... jamais*, and so on.
- ★ Use relative pronouns and conjunctions.
- ★ Know the irregular verbs.

### Nouns and pronouns

- ★ Use the correct type of article/determiner (a, the, this), and the correct form (e.g. correct gender or number).
- ★ Use the correct pronouns, and put them in the right place.
- ★ Use the correct plural forms.

# How do I go about learning vocabulary?

The best way to revise is to practise. Although different people have different ways of learning vocabulary, the following ways might be useful to you:

## Hints & tips ⭐

✓ Try writing down a list of words, then reading them out loud. Cover up the French words, and see if you can remember them from the English, and of course the other way round.

✓ Read vocabulary/texts over several times, on different occasions.

✓ Check your memorising, by either covering one part and remembering the other, or by getting someone (a friend or a parent) to do it with you. If you have someone who will help you, get them to say a word in English, which you have to put into French.

✓ Try to get your words organised into areas, so they all hang together and make sense to you.

✓ Use spidergrams of related words.

Appendix 1 gives an overview of all the topic areas that might come up, and in Chapter 12 you will find both basic vocabulary and vocabulary that you might come across in each of the four contexts of Society, Learning, Employability and Culture.

## What you should be able to do

* Use a dictionary quickly and effectively (not just an electronic dictionary).
* Skim and read for the gist of a passage.
* Read the questions carefully.
* Use the questions to guide your answers.
* Answer quickly and concisely.
* Manage your time effectively.

## Remember

☞ Verbs are the key to understanding a passage.
☞ Make sure you can identify the verbs in a sentence.
☞ Know how to use the verb pages in a dictionary to identify tenses and different forms of the verb.

# Introduction

Answering the questions in your Reading paper is worth 20 marks; you will also have to translate a short passage from the text you read into English, for a further 10 marks. The text will be about 600 words long. You will be able to use a dictionary for this exam, and so you need to be very confident in your dictionary use.

When you sit the exam, you will have two hours for the paper, which has Directed writing as well as Reading and translation. It is up to you how to divide the time, and what order to do the two papers in. There is more guidance on this in Chapter 10 (Directed writing). However, if you spend an hour on the Directed writing, as a rough guideline you should spend around 50 minutes on the reading and about 10 minutes on the translation. You can start off with either the reading or directed writing section. Some people prefer to start off with the translation, to 'get it out the way', but it is a much better plan to leave the translation till after you have finished the questions, as you are likely to have a deeper understanding of the text by then, and will find that a help with the translation. The translation is a short passage, broken into five chunks for marking, and you will get a mark out of two for each chunk.

Just as at National 5, you do not have to understand all of the text thoroughly for most of the questions: you have to get the gist of the text, and then identify carefully the location of the answers you need, taking more time with these areas of the text. The final question, worth two marks, will require you to have an overall understanding of what the text is about, but again you do not have to understand every word to have a feeling for the overall meaning.

Reading is a skill, and a skill you need to work on to allow you to give of your best in the final exam. You are not expected to give every detail, or translate word for word what is in the French text. Sometimes the details will matter, but what is more important is that you demonstrate you have understood what the text is about, and put your answers into good English. If your answers do not make sense, then you can assume they are wrong! You do not have to answer in sentences, but be careful not to give answers that are too short.

There is a sequence you should follow:

1  Read the information in English about the text at the start: this should give you clues as to what the answers are going to be about. Now look quickly at the questions: they should give you a good clue as to what the passage is about, and help you when you skim it for the first time. Notice also that just above the questions you may find a glossary of words, which will save you having to look up these words in a dictionary.

2  Only now should you look at the text: skim through it to get an idea of what it is about, without using a dictionary. This is a challenging task, as you will want to look up words all the time, but resist the temptation for the first run through.

3  Now go back to the questions, and start looking for where the answers are in the passage. Remember that the questions will follow the same order as the text, and you should not have to jump around all over the place. There will also be line references at the start of each question to help you know where to look. Use a highlighter pen, or underline the chunks of text you think are relevant. Remember to watch how many marks each question is worth, as a clue to how much to put in your answer.

4  This is when your dictionary will come into play. But be very careful: it is easy to look up far too many words, and end up with not enough time to finish the paper. Get into a pattern when trying to understand a piece of text:

   ● Identify the verbs in the sentence, and look these words up if you do not know them (watch for irregular endings!).
   ● Identify the subjects of the verbs: these might be pronouns, so know who or what they are referring back to, or nouns, in which case make sure you know what these mean.
   ● Once you have the subjects and verbs, the sentences should make more sense, and it is easier to work out what else you need to know.

*Hints & tips* ★

✓ *Always read the questions before you look at a passage: they give a good guide to the content.*
✓ *Read through the passage the first time without a dictionary to get a feel for what it is about.*

# Sample Reading paper

Let us look at a past Higher Reading paper, and see how the sequence will work in practice. We will give you the passage, and the questions, but also provide some guidance on how to answer. Read the article carefully, then answer in **English** the questions that follow. The translation will be a short passage from the text. For guidance on the translation, go to the chapter on translation (Chapter 2).

*In this article you will read about how French attitudes to holidays have changed.*

# Le Français en vacances : ce qui a changé

Sur les bords de la Méditerranée, à Saint-Tropez ou ailleurs, le vacancier arrive. Il a des sandales aux pieds et il marche sur le sable chaud des plages surpeuplées. <u>Comme l'année dernière et les années précédentes, il a réservé des chambres dans un bel</u>
5 <u>hôtel pas trop loin de la plage. Les enfants vont jouer dans la mer pendant que maman passe la journée à se bronzer et que papa boit du vin avec le voisin.</u>

## Les destinations ont changé

Voilà l'image du passé. Maintenant le vacancier ne se lance plus vers le sud, le sable et la chaleur. Il cherche plutôt la campagne,
10 la randonnée et les gîtes ruraux. La France est devenue, aux yeux des vacanciers, un patchwork magique de petits chemins et de paysages fleuris. Beaucoup préfèrent choisir maintenant les bords de rivière ou les petits villages silencieux loin des grandes routes au lieu des plages pleines de corps très bronzés.

15 Il ne faudrait pas croire cependant que les vacanciers ont déserté la côte française. Il y en a toujours des centaines de milliers qui **se ruent*** dans les stations balnéaires. Mais le Français est aujourd'hui un peu plus exigeant : il veut que l'eau de mer soit claire et non-polluée. D'où la popularité de plus en plus marquée
20 de la Bretagne. Elle est devenue la deuxième destination française des Français après la Côte D'Azur.

## Les loisirs ont changé

En plus, les loisirs des Français ont changé en même temps que leurs destinations. Ils ne veulent plus les sports violents comme le squash, le jogging et autres tortures qui font mal partout.
25 Les nouveaux vacanciers redécouvrent les plaisirs beaucoup plus paisibles de la marche à pied, excellente recette pour le maintien de la forme et la prévention des accidents cardiovasculaires. Ils continuent à aimer faire du vélo.

Sur les plages, **hors-bord*** et autres scooters des mers ne sont plus
30 populaires. Ils sont trop bruyants, trop pollueurs pour ne pas dire trop dangereux pour le vacancier qui cherche le calme. Le nouveau passetemps, c'est de construire et de peindre son propre bateau.

Très en vogue aussi, tous les articles et les vêtements des vacances à la campagne. Les tentes, sacs à dos, sacs de couchage, thermos,
35 blousons confortables aux couleurs camouflage.

## La mode a changé

La mode aussi a subi des changements. Finis les transistors et les maillots de bain fluorescents. Sur la plage, la femme à la mode porte cet été une tenue moins frappante, toujours bleue.

⇨

Ses vêtements se sont féminisés. Elle se promène avec un sac
40 en paille sur l'épaule et, sur le nez, elle a posé des lunettes avec
montures interchangeables qu'elle peut assortir à son T-shirt.

Son compagnon est lui aussi devenu plus sobre. Maintenant, il
porte des vêtements en fibres naturelles, et il aime le style sportif
américain, avec des T-shirts XXL, extra-extra larges, qui laissent
45 une impression de liberté. Seule fantaisie : un bandana corsaire
sur la tête. S'il porte des lunettes, elles sont rondes à la Lennon,
noires ou en écaille. Mais surtout pas (quelle horreur !) colorées.

### La façon de se bronzer a changé

Et puis, si l'on veut vraiment bronzer, il faut le faire intelligemment,
en bougeant et non pas bêtement étendu sur son drap de bain.
50 Toujours très en vogue : le frisbee et le badminton. Tout nouveau,
en revanche : le scatch, un jeu tout simple qui consiste à envoyer
une balle que le partenaire rattrape avec un petit disque couvert
de Velcro.

Pourquoi le vacancier français a-t-il fait tous ces changements ?
55 Alors il y a un peu de tout. L'amour de son pays, le désir d'être
plus écologiste, la recherche d'un nouvel art de vivre.

### Glossary

se ruer (dans): *to dash (into)*

un hors-bord: *speedboat*

## Question ?

Re-read lines 8–21.

1 French people have changed where they choose to go.
   a) In what way has their choice of destination changed? Give details. **2**

   ..................................................................................................................................

   ..................................................................................................................................

*You are asked to give details about how things have changed: there are
two marks, so go for before and after: you are told where to look, and you
can then find in the passage that* le vacancier ne se lance plus: *subject and
verb mean the holidaymaker no longer dashes: (watch that reflexive verb!)
towards the south, sun and heat. The passage then goes on* Il cherche, *that
is, he looks for...*

## Question ❓

**b)** What do many people now prefer? State **three** things.  **3**

.........................................................................................................................................................................

.........................................................................................................................................................................

.........................................................................................................................................................................

*The question says 'State **three** things', so after 'prefer' you should find three things to mention. The magic word to look for is* préfèrent, *as this is the value judgement.*

## Question ❓

**c)** Why has Brittany become even more popular?  **1**

.........................................................................................................................................................................

*You can find* popularité *and* la Bretagne *easily. A little trick here:* D'où *means 'that is why', so the answer is just before this.*

## Question ❓

Re-read lines 22–32.

**2**  Holiday activities have also changed.
   **a)**  Which kinds of activities are no longer popular? Give details.  **1**

.........................................................................................................................................................................

*One mark, but the question asks for 'activities' in the plural, so mention them all! If in doubt when answering a question, give details, as long as you are sure they are correct.*

## Question ❓

**b)** What do holidaymakers now prefer to do? State any **one** thing.  **1**

.........................................................................................................................................................................

*This means there is more than one answer, so choose the one you find easier, and move on to the next question; you don't need to find more than one answer.*

## Question ?

c) What has changed for holidaymakers who go to the beach? Why is this the case?  **2**

........................................................................................................................................................

........................................................................................................................................................

*One answer, but make sure you include the detail, and give a reason as well for the second mark.*

## Question ?

Re-read lines 36–47

3 Fashionable holidaymakers have also changed their style of dress.
   a) In what way has women's dress changed? State any **three** things.  **3**

........................................................................................................................................................

........................................................................................................................................................

........................................................................................................................................................

*Any three means there are more than three, so again, choose the three you find easiest then move on. If you are not sure of your answer, you can give four, hoping three are right! Look for what they used to be like and what they are like now; go for details, but do not translate the whole paragraph, as you are looking for only three marks.*

## Question ?

b) What are the main features of men's holiday wear? State any **three** things.  **3**

........................................................................................................................................................

........................................................................................................................................................

........................................................................................................................................................

*Three marks so give as many details as you can; there are, however, more than three things possible, so choose the three that you can get with least guessing/use of the dictionary. Do not waste time!*

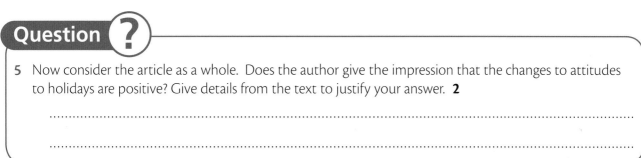

**Question** **?**

Re-read lines 48–53

4  The attitude to sunbathing has changed. What has been the result of these changes? State **two** things.  **2**

..................................................................................................................................................................

..................................................................................................................................................................

*The question asks for two things, so no choice here; again, go for before
and after, remember the verb rule, and notice that* bougeant *and* étendu
*are verbs!*

 **Question** **?**

5  Now consider the article as a whole.  Does the author give the impression that the changes to attitudes
to holidays are positive? Give details from the text to justify your answer.  **2**

..................................................................................................................................................................

..................................................................................................................................................................

*For this answer, it is important that you make a decision, and then state
it: the author gives the impression that... Start off with your statement,
then quote some pieces of evidence from the text (in English!) which justify
your decision. Two justifications should be enough.*

**Question** **?**

6  Translate into English:
   Comme l'année dernière et les années précédentes, il a réservé des chambres dans un bel hôtel pas trop
   loin de la plage. Les enfants vont jouer dans la mer pendant que maman passe la journée à se bronzer et
   que papa boit du vin avec le voisin.

*See Chapter 2 for guidance on this question.*

# Marking scheme

1  a) They used to go to the south for sand and heat/Now they go for the country, walks and cottages  **2**

b) Riversides (banks)/Quiet little villages/Far from the overfilled beaches  **3**

c) It has clear, unpolluted water  **1**

2  a) Energetic (violent) sports like squash and jogging  **1**

b) Walking to keep fit/Going cycling (any one)  **1**

c) Speedboats and water scooters are no longer popular/They are too noisy, polluting and dangerous  **2**

3  a) No more fluorescent swimsuits/Clothes are less garish (striking)/ Clothes are more feminine/A straw bag over the shoulder/ Sunglasses with frames to match tops (any three)  **3**

b) Clothing in natural fibres/American sport style with XXL T-shirts/ Perhaps a bandana on the head (pirate style)/Round sunglasses in metal or tortoiseshell (any three)  **3**

4  It is done intelligently doing activities like frisbee or badminton/No longer just lying on a towel  **2**

5  The author is positive about the changes; he talks about:
- the magic patchwork of flowery landscapes
- the overcrowded beaches that used to be popular
- holidaymakers have become more demanding
- the activities people used to do as 'violent' and torture
- new activities are excellent for fitness and health
- old water activities were dangerous and polluting
- people sunbathe more intelligently
- people want to be more green  **2**

6  See Chapter 2 for guidance and marking scheme for this question.

## What you should be able to do

★ Use a dictionary quickly and effectively (not just an electronic dictionary).
★ Check you have included everything.

## Hints & tips

✓ Give yourself time to do justice to the translation; it is worth 10 marks, so 10 minutes are well spent.
✓ Consider tackling the translation before the overall purpose question, which is only worth two marks but will take up some time.

# Introduction

After answering the questions in your Reading paper, you will also have to translate a short passage from the text you read into English, for a further **10 marks**.

When you sit the exam, you will have two hours for the paper, which contains reading, translation and the directed writing. It is up to you how to divide the time, and what order to do the paper in, but as a rough guideline you should spend around 50 minutes on the reading, 10 minutes on the translation and 40 minutes on the directed writing. This gives you 20 minutes to add to any area you feel needs extra time. Some people prefer to start off with the translation, to 'get it out the way', but it is a much better plan to leave the translation till after you have finished the questions, as you are likely to have a deeper understanding of the text by then, and will find that a help with the translation. You might also spend a long time on the translation at the start of the exam, and not have enough time to answer all the questions. You might, however, tackle the translation before the final 'overall purpose' question. The translation is a short passage, broken into five sense units for marking, and you will earn a mark for each sense unit. As the translation into English is allocated 10 marks, each sense unit is worth two marks, which will be awarded according to the quality and accuracy of the translation into English. In assessing performance, the descriptions below will be used. Each sense unit will be awarded one of the marks shown.

| Good | 2 | Essential information and relevant details are understood and conveyed clearly and accurately, with appropriate use of English. |
| Satisfactory | 1 | Essential information is understood and conveyed clearly and comprehensibly, although some of the details may be translated in an imprecise or inaccurate manner. The key message is conveyed in spite of inaccuracies and weaknesses in the use of English. |
| Unsatisfactory | 0 | The candidate fails to demonstrate sufficient understanding of the essential information. |

# Sample translation question

Let's revisit the sample Higher Reading paper from Chapter 1, and see how this will work in practice. The translation is a short passage from the text discussing holidays, *Le Français en vacances : ce qui a changé.*

## Question ?

8    Translate into English:

Comme l'année dernière et les années précédentes, il a réservé des chambres dans un bel hôtel pas trop loin de la plage. Les enfants vont jouer dans la mer pendant que maman passe la journée à se bronzer et que papa boit du vin avec le voisin.

Let us break this down into the five units that will be marked, with two marks for each section.

1    Comme l'année dernière et les années précédentes,
2    il a réservé des chambres dans un bel hôtel pas trop loin de la plage.
3    Les enfants vont jouer dans la mer
4    pendant que maman passe la journée à se bronzer
5    et que papa boit du vin avec le voisin.

Unlike the reading questions, it is important that you understand every detail here, and that you transmit the message the author was giving in French. Make sure you get the verb tenses right!

1    For the first unit, make sure you get the correct translation of *comme*, one which makes sense, and remember to put the adjectives in front of the nouns.
2    For the second unit, make sure you put in every word, apart from *des*, which we can do without in English.
3    In the third unit, the trick is to get the correct tense of the verb.
4    In the fourth unit, watch out for the reflexive verb when using a dictionary.
5    The last unit has a couple of words in it which we do not need in English, and would make the translation wrong if we included them.

Now try to translate the passage, and then check your answer against the sample paper translation at the end of this chapter (p.13). The marking scheme for this is very straightforward, and does not give us an idea of what a marking scheme in a real exam will look like.

As the translation is worth 10 marks, and the questions 20, make sure you leave yourself enough time to do the translation justice. That should mean about ten minutes, normally. Here is part of the marking scheme from an older Higher, to show you how a sense unit is marked. Have a look at it, and see what a number of different possibilities there are for answers, and what you would lose marks for. The original text for translation was:

Encouragés par le succès de cette jeune New-Yorkaise, des centaines de « Mendiants d'Internet » ont créé des sites simplement pour faire appel à la générosité des autres. Chacun a une histoire à raconter qui a pour but d'attirer notre compassion.

This is the first sense unit:

| Text | Good<br>2 | Satisfactory<br>1 | Unsatisfactory<br>0 |
|---|---|---|---|
| Encouragés par le succès de cette jeune New-Yorkaise,<br><br>Encouragés<br><br>par le succès<br><br>de cette<br><br>jeune New Yorkaise | Encouraged by the success of this/that young New Yorker/girl from NY,<br><br>Encouraged<br><br>by the success<br><br>of this/that<br><br>young NewYorker/young girl from New York<br><br>young person/woman/ youngster from New York<br><br>young inhabitant of New York | through the success<br><br>the successes<br><br>the<br><br>youth/teenager<br><br>New Yorkian | By encouraging<br><br>To be encouraged<br><br>Encouragement<br><br>these/those<br><br>child<br><br>omission of 'young' (except with 'girl')<br><br>New Yorkshire<br><br>New Yorkaise<br><br>New Yorker<u>s</u><br><br>young people from New York |

Notice if you miss out 'young', you lose both marks. Making a mistake between singular and plural also loses you both marks. The translation here should be more or less word for word. However, the last sense unit is different:

| Text | Good<br>2 | Satisfactory<br>1 |
|---|---|---|
| qui a pour but d'attirer notre compassion.<br><br>qui a pour but<br><br>d'attirer<br><br>notre compassion. | with the aim of attracting our compassion.<br><br>that/which aims to<br><br>whose aim/goal is to<br><br>which is aimed at<br><br>the purpose/intention of which is<br><br>with the aim/objective of<br><br>(to) attract/(of) attracting<br><br>(to) arouse/engage<br><br>our compassion/sympathy/pity | to/in order to<br><br>(to) entice<br><br>(to) lure<br><br>(to) incite<br><br>(to) gain/win<br><br>(to) appeal to<br><br>(to) draw<br><br>your |

The French literally says 'which has for goal to attract our compassion', which of course makes no sense in English, so we have to change it around to make sense in English. Getting right what you should leave and what you should change is the hardest part of doing a translation. Practice will make you better at this. Try to translate the rest of the extract:

> des centaines de « Mendiants d'Internet » ont créé des sites simplement pour faire appel à la générosité des autres. Chacun a une histoire à raconter

Note that *mendiant* means 'beggar'. The suggested answer is at the end of this chapter (p.13).

# Guidance

The rules for understanding the French in order to make a translation are the same as for answering questions: look for the verbs first, find the subjects of these verbs and the rest should fall into place more easily. There are some differences here, however. You need to give **all** the details; you must answer in sentences if the original is in sentences; and you have to get details just right. It is no good getting the right verb, for instance, but the wrong tense.

There are some important points to remember.

## *Remember*

☞ *If what you have written does not make sense in English, then it is guaranteed to be wrong.*

⇨

⇨
☞ Make sure you use the correct tense of the verb.
☞ Do not miss out any adjectives or adverbs: it is easy to forget a little word, and most marks are lost this way.
☞ Missing out one word can lose you both marks for that sense unit: check afterwards that you have included everything, perhaps by striking out the words on the question paper.
☞ You do not have to do a word-for-word translation: translate the sense of the original into English with all details in place.

Try translating small chunks of text from any passage you read to get into the habit of translating, and discuss your answers with others. Another useful task is to take a piece of French text and run it through a translation machine or site on the internet such as Babelfish or Google Language tools. This will give you a translation that will probably be in bad English, and will not always make sense. Try to make it make sense in English, looking at the original and coming up with a proper translation. This will develop your attention to detail, and help you think about the quality of the English in your answer. And remember, if you put your own English text into a translation machine, and ask it to translate it into French, the result might well be in bad French and not always make sense!

# Sample paper translation

*Comme l'année dernière et les années précédentes,*

Like last year and the years before,

*il a réservé des chambres dans un bel hôtel pas trop loin de la plage.*

he reserved rooms in a nice hotel not too far from the beach.

*Les enfants vont jouer dans la mer*

The children go and play in the sea

*pendant que maman passe la journée à se bronzer*

while mum spends the day getting a tan/sunbathing

*et que papa boit du vin avec le voisin.*

and dad drinks wine with the neighbour.

# Past paper translation

Encouraged by the success of this girl from New York, hundreds of 'Internet Beggars' have created sites simply to appeal to the generosity of others/other people. Each one has a story to tell with the aim of attracting our compassion.

# Introduction

You would normally be expected to complete these reading assessments in a time of about 50 minutes. You are allowed a dictionary. For the translation, allow another 10 minutes. You do not need to answer the first questions in sentences. However, make sure your answers give enough details. The last question will be a bit longer, and might be best with a sentence followed by some bullet points.

Here are four examples of reading passages for you to practise with.

## Example 1

*You read this article about people meeting up on the internet.*

*Remember*

☞ Check how many marks a question is worth; this lets you know how many details to give.

☞ You do not have to write in sentences; phrases or bullet points are enough.

## La vogue des rencontres sur Internet

Près de 4 millions de Français fréquentent chaque jour les sites de rencontres sur Internet. Hommes, femmes, jeunes et moins jeunes : tous espèrent y trouver l'amour …

Il est 21 heures. Léo, 4 ans, et Élisa, 8 ans, sont couchés. Leur maman
5  peut souffler. « Je mange un petit quelque chose et je commence. »
Deux fois par semaine, le mardi et le vendredi, Patricia, 32 ans,
prof de maths dans un collège de Nantes, devient *La Reine des Fées*.
Jusqu'à minuit, elle part à la rencontre d'inconnus avec qui elle
**papote**\*, discute, échange des messages …

10  Pourquoi s'inscrire sur un site de rencontre ? La réponse commune
à cette question est bien d'avoir le désir de connaître de nouvelles
personnes afin d'en faire son ou sa partenaire durable ou à des fins
⇨

⇨

de multiplication de rencontres, de rompre une solitude pesante ou
tout simplement le besoin de découvrir des nouvelles personnes
15  puisque le Web nous en donne l'occasion facilement. Patricia
fait partie de ces millions de Français qui se connectent chaque
jour sur un des nombreux sites de rencontres sur Internet. Ces
sites s'appellent Meetic, Net Club, Match, Se rencontrer … Leur
objectif : mettre en contact les personnes seules, leur permettre de
20  communiquer en direct par messages. Et le marché est immense : la
France compte environ 12 millions de célibataires. Un Français sur
cinq vit seul ! Et tous ces gens rêvent de soirées qui ressemblent à
autre chose qu'un tête-à-tête avec la télé.

25  Est-il possible de rencontrer l'amour sur Internet ? Est-ce la dernière
mode en date pour les **branchés**\* des grandes villes, ou est-ce
que cela fonctionne ? Ce n'est certainement pas une mode. C'est
un phénomène de société, un changement dans le comportement
des solitaires. Ce qui était inconcevable il y a dix ans est en train de
30  devenir le premier mode de rencontre, avant le travail ou les soirées
entre amis. Patricia a découvert le site de rencontres Match en
janvier dernier : « Je sortais très malheureuse d'un divorce difficile,
persuadée que je ne trouverais jamais le bonheur. Entre mon travail
de professeur et mes deux enfants, je n'ai pas le temps de sortir,
encore moins de rencontrer des amis nouveaux. »

35  Une collègue lui confie avoir rencontré son mari sur Internet.
« D'abord j'ai trouvé ça ridicule. » Mais quelques jours plus tard
elle regarde le site elle-même. « Comme c'était gratuit, je me suis
inscrite. J'ai rempli ma **fiche signalétique**\* et le lendemain des
hommes m'ont proposé de dialoguer avec eux. »

40  Tout nouvel inscrit sur un site de rencontres doit choisir un
pseudonyme et remplir une « fiche ». On y apprend que Patricia, alias
*La Reine des Fées*, a les yeux couleur noisette, les cheveux blonds
coupés court, deux enfants, un penchant pour les restaurants italiens
et les films à suspense, déteste les hommes arrogants, pratique la
45  randonnée … et rêve encore de rencontrer le grand amour.

Que faut-il faire pour s'inscrire ? Pas grand-chose … cela prend
2 minutes, montre en main. Choisir un pseudo qui colle à votre
personnalité, avoir une adresse mail valide (une spécialement créée
pour ça est préférable), en effet, il n'est pas conseillé de mettre son
50  adresse mail personnelle qui sert aux amis et à la famille, pas plus
qu'une adresse professionnelle. Vous pouvez en créer une chez votre
opérateur, Orange, Free, SFR etc. ou sur live.fr, yahoo.fr, gmail.com
et bien d'autres. Le site où vous vous serez inscrit va simplement
vous demander la confirmation de votre inscription par mail.

*Glossary*

| papoter | *to chat* |
| branché | *up-to-the-minute person* |
| fiche signalétique | *personal information form* |

## Questions ?

This article describes how French people use the internet to find partners.

Re-read lines 4–9.

1 Patricia has started to use the internet to meet people.
   a) When exactly does she do this? Give details. **3**

   ......................................................................................................................................................

   ......................................................................................................................................................

   ......................................................................................................................................................

   b) Who does she chat to? **1**

   ......................................................................................................................................................

Re-read lines 10–23.

2 We learn why people go on to the chat sites.
   a) Can you give any **two** reasons? **2**

   ......................................................................................................................................................

   ......................................................................................................................................................

   b) What do the chat sites hope to do? **2**

   ......................................................................................................................................................

   ......................................................................................................................................................

   c) Why have so many people started to go on to this kind of site? **2**

   ......................................................................................................................................................

   ......................................................................................................................................................

Re-read lines 24–30.

3 The author suggests this may just be for very fashionable people.
   a) Does he agree? Give a reason for your answer. **1**

   ......................................................................................................................................................

   b) What were the usual ways of meeting people previously? **2**

   ......................................................................................................................................................

   ......................................................................................................................................................

Re-read lines 35–45.

4 Patricia explains how she got started with online chatting.
   a) In what way did she first hear about it? **1**

   ......................................................................................................................................................

   b) What is Patricia looking for? **1**

   ......................................................................................................................................................

Re-read lines 46–51.

5 We learn how to sign up for one of these sites.
   a) What should we choose? **1**

   ......................................................................................................................................................

   b) What **two** things should we not use? **2**

   ......................................................................................................................................................

   ......................................................................................................................................................

⇒

⇨

**6** Now consider the article as a whole. Does the author give the impression that using meeting sites is a positive step? Give details from the text to justify your answer. **2**

...................................................................................................................................................

...................................................................................................................................................

Total **20**

**7** Now translate lines 31–34 (Je … nouveaux.).

# Example 2

*This article discusses the system in France where children are often asked to repeat a year.*

## Scolarité : le redoublement est-il un échec ?

Des études statistiques menées en France ont montré qu'en moyenne, chaque année, plus de 60 000 élèves sont victimes de redoublement. Le redoublement scolaire est-il nécessaire ou non ? Voilà la question fondamentale que se posent les parents et les
5 enseignants d'aujourd'hui. Suites à des études statistiques, sur un échantillon de 1000 individus, dont parents et enseignants, 65 % des parents et 58 % des enseignants enquêtés déclarent être pour le redoublement des élèves. Ainsi, selon ces derniers, c'est le meilleur moyen pour aider les enfants en difficulté. Toutefois, pour
10 certains, redoubler est une perte de temps. En effet, il constitue plutôt une sorte de démotivation pour les élèves qu'une aide. Des études comparatives entre plusieurs pays ont montré que les pays qui affichent un taux de redoublement élevé sont beaucoup moins performants, sur le plan éducatif, que ceux dont le taux est faible.

15 Dans quelle mesure un redoublement peut-il être positif ? <u>Le redoublement peut être une chance pour l'élève qui a connu un drame dans sa vie (une mort dans la famille, par exemple) et pour celui qui a un niveau scolaire un peu juste mais fait néanmoins des efforts pour avoir de meilleurs résultats.</u> Valérie Sultan, professeur

⇨

⇨

20 principal en classe de troisième, raconte qu'un redoublement n'est pas forcément synonyme d'échec. Au contraire, il peut permettre à l'enfant de repartir sur des bases nouvelles. Mais faire redoubler un élève, c'est toujours un pari. Elle parle aussi par exemple d'un enfant de sixième qui éprouve des difficultés à s'adapter

25 à l'enseignement du collège, ou à un adolescent qui, en pleine transformation physique et psychologique, est préoccupé par autre chose que l'école et a besoin de respirer quelques mois. Mais il est important de se souvenir du fait que, pour que le redoublement soit une chance, il ne faut pas le présenter comme une punition.

30 Faut-il **faire le forcing**\* pour faire passer son enfant dans la classe supérieure ? Il est toujours préférable de discuter d'abord avec l'école. Conseillers d'orientation et professeurs travaillent tous dans l'intérêt de l'élève. Lorsqu'on est parent, on a une relation intime avec son enfant. Du coup, on ne voit pas

35 forcément la réalité, et on peut se tromper. Les enseignants peuvent avoir davantage de distance. Valérie Sultan raconte que, lors des rencontres parents–professeurs, les profs sont ainsi capables de repérer que le désir de l'un n'est pas forcément celui de l'autre : par exemple, les parents veulent absolument que leur enfant fasse une

40 seconde générale avec l'intention de préparer le bac scientifique, alors que l'élève a un autre projet en tête.

Valérie Sultan pense qu'il y a des classes où il est préférable de ne pas contester le redoublement. Ce sont les classes « importantes » : la sixième et la quatrième, au cours de laquelle les élèves

45 apprennent une seconde langue vivante. Quant à la troisième, après avoir évalué le niveau des élèves à la fin de leur temps en collège, les écoles ne retiennent le redoublement que pour une petite partie d'entre eux. On propose que les autres adolescents en difficulté soient orientés vers un lycée professionnel. Dans

50 les classes de sixième, quatrième et troisième, ce sont tous les professeurs de la classe qui décident de faire passer ou redoubler l'enfant. Si la famille veut contester son choix, elle est obligée de faire appel. En cinquième, c'est différent : les professeurs donnent des conseils sur l'orientation. C'est la famille qui prend la décision finale.

*Glossary*

faire le forcing                    *put on pressure*

## Questions ❓

Re-read lines 1–14.

1   The article starts with an overview of the system.

   a) What statistics does the article give about repeating a year in France?  **3**

   .......................................................................................................................................

   .......................................................................................................................................

   .......................................................................................................................................

   ⇨

⇨

**b)** What negative effect might repeating a year have on children? **1**

........................................................................................................................

**c)** What do comparative studies in different countries show? **1**

........................................................................................................................

Re-read lines 19–29.

2 Mme Sultan talks about in what way repeating a year can be positive.
  **a)** Why might it be a good chance for a pupil? **1**

........................................................................................................................

  **b)** She mentions two further cases where it could be advisable. Give details. **2**

........................................................................................................................

........................................................................................................................

  **c)** What is it important to bear in mind? **1**

........................................................................................................................

Re-read lines 30–41.

3 We learn about the danger of putting too much pressure on the pupil.
  **a)** What should parents do? **1**

........................................................................................................................

  **b)** Why should they do this? **2**

........................................................................................................................

........................................................................................................................

  **c)** When does Mme Sultan notice that parents do not always see things correctly? **1**

........................................................................................................................

  **d)** What do teachers often notice? **2**

........................................................................................................................

........................................................................................................................

Re-read lines 42–54.

4 In some classes parents should just accept that their child should repeat the year, according
  to Mme Sultan.
  **a)** Why do very few students repeat *troisième* (fourth year)? **2**

........................................................................................................................

........................................................................................................................

  **b)** What is different about the situation in *cinquième* (second year)? **1**

........................................................................................................................

5 Now consider the article as a whole. Do the authors give the impression that they are in
  favour of repeating, against it, or trying to give a balanced view? Give details from the text
  to justify your answer. **2**

........................................................................................................................

........................................................................................................................

Total **20**

6 Now translate lines 15–19 (Le … résultats.).

# Example 3

*This article discusses the pressures fashion puts on people.*

## La mode du sport : les baskets et les jogging !

On est en 1986. Les dirigeants de la marque aux trois bandes signent avec Run DMC le premier contrat non-sportif de l'histoire du marchand du sport : un million de dollars. Dans un seul weekend, il se vend pour 22 millions de dollars de produits siglés
5  Adidas–Run DMC. Aujourd'hui, 79 % des jeunes Français de 8 à 19 ans, quand ils pensent à des marques de vêtements, citent des griffes de sport. Stella McCartney **fait un malheur*** chez Adidas depuis qu'elle y dessine une collection. Une génération d'urbains adeptes du « cool » se retrouve dans les modèles de Puma, qui
10 collabore avec Philippe Starck ou Alexander McQueen.

Les trois grandes marques Nike, Adidas et Puma sont en train de quitter le sport pour la mode. <u>Jusqu'à présent, pour les marques de sport, toute leur énergie était consacrée à la technologie et la performance. Les femmes, qui ne représentent que 30 % de la</u>
15 <u>clientèle, constituent « le » marché de demain. Avant, on prenait les vêtements pour hommes, on les taillait plus courts et plus étroits et voilà, c'était la ligne féminine.</u>

Un responsable du style chez Nike à Portland (Oregon, États-Unis) peut-il séduire une consommatrice parisienne devouée à la mode ?
20 Pas vraiment. Les Américains pensent encore que les filles, c'est du rose et blanc porté assez large, quand les Londoniennes ou Parisiennes ont adopté jeans serrés et look rock. Les dirigeants de Nike ont pris en compte l'existence du consommateur mode. Conséquence : on a recruté en Europe des dénicheurs de
25 tendances dont la mission est d'envoyer à Portland des comptes rendus réguliers sur l'évolution des modes dans la rue.

⇨

⇨

On va s'orienter vers la mode, oui, et vers les femmes, c'est certain, mais avec des stylistes maison. Après tout, l'entreprise au Swoosh est l'une des plus grandes employeuses de designers au monde.

30 Contrairement aux Allemandes (des sportives sérieuses) ou aux Britanniques (des fanatiques de running), les Françaises sont avant tout folles de style. À elles les collections de Stella McCartney, petits **hauts**\* couleur taupe et bas de jogging serrés. Les gens d'Adidas ont fait le même calcul que ceux de Nike : les
35 femmes ! Et pour les conquérir il faut insister sur le côté mode et style, à la différence des acheteurs hommes, qui sont encore centrés sur le sport.

La collaboration de Stella McCartney avec la marque est née un jour de 2000 lors d'une table ronde réunissant, autour des
40 collaborateurs d'Adidas, des créateurs venus parler style. Et Stella, qui est une sportive (natation, yoga), a pu dire : « Pourquoi est-on obligées de ressembler à des sacs ? » Depuis, elle et ses collaborateurs londoniens travaillent avec le bureau de style d'Adidas, en Allemagne.

45 Quant à Puma, quoi alors ? Voilà la description de l'acheteur type Puma : « Ce n'est pas forcément le mec le plus beau, le meilleur, mais c'est le plus cool, et sa copine est la mieux. » Car, avec des bureaux de style à Londres, Boston et à Herzogenaurach, plus de 100 personnes en tout, sans compter une cellule « sport fashion »
50 d'une cinquantaine de designers à Londres, Puma se trouve branché. « Les coupes sont près du corps, les matières légères, les shorts descendent aux genoux, même nos étiquettes sont rigolotes. »

Qui inventera l'équivalent du sweat à capuche du XXIe siècle ?
55 Une chose est certaine : les marques de sport font la jonction entre les différents styles et looks de la rue. Le vintage, toujours ; les sports « *porteurs d'image* » (surf, skate) bien sûr ; et les collections femmes, évidemment. Dans le textile, les hauts se vendent mieux que les bas, car le jeans joue désormais le rôle du casual. Le
60 jackpot reviendra à la marque qui inventera de quoi habiller les femmes en bas. Trois, deux, un, partez !

*Glossary*

| | |
|---|---|
| faire un malheur | *be a smash hit, great success* |
| un haut | *a top (article of clothing)* |

## Questions ❓

This article describes how important fashion is to sports clothes in France.

Re-read lines 1–10.

**1** We read some background information.
   **a)** Why are the rap group Run DMC mentioned? **2**

   .............................................................................................................................................

   .............................................................................................................................................

   **b)** What statistic do we learn about young French people? **1**

   .............................................................................................................................................

Re-read lines 18–28.

**2** We read how Nike is dealing with the issue.
   **a)** In what way do young Americans and young French girls differ in their approach to fashion? **2**

   .............................................................................................................................................

   .............................................................................................................................................

   **b)** What are Nike doing about this? **2**

   .............................................................................................................................................

   .............................................................................................................................................

Re-read lines 30–44.

**3** The author talks about Adidas.
   **a)** What Adidas products do young French girls like? **2**

   .............................................................................................................................................

   .............................................................................................................................................

   **b)** What differences between male and female customers are noticed? **2**

   .............................................................................................................................................

   .............................................................................................................................................

   **c)** The article describes how Stella McCartney came to work with Adidas. Give **two** details of this. **2**

   .............................................................................................................................................

   .............................................................................................................................................

Re-read lines 45–53.

**4** We learn about Puma's involvement in sports fashion.
   What description does Puma give of their average male customer? **3**

   .............................................................................................................................................

   .............................................................................................................................................

   .............................................................................................................................................

Re-read lines 54–59.

**5** The author looks to the future.
   **a)** What question does the author ask? **1**

   .............................................................................................................................................

   **b)** Why do sports tops sell better than sports trousers? **1**

   .............................................................................................................................................

⇨

⇨

**6** Now consider the article as a whole. Does the author give the impression that he is in favour of or against sporting fashion? Give details from the text to justify your answer. **2**

.......................................................................................................................................................

.......................................................................................................................................................

Total **20**

**7** Now translate lines 12–17 (Jusqu'à présent … la ligne féminine.).

## Example 4

*You come across this article about texting.*

# SMS, textos : dites « Je t'M » avec le pouce !

<u>En quelques années, les mini-messages ou SMS ont conquis tous les propriétaires de mobile ! À tel point que le pouce est devenu un organe de communication à part entière. Qui aujourd'hui envoie encore une lettre d'amour par la poste pour la Saint-Valentin ? Un</u>
5 <u>message texte suffit</u> !

Plus de quatre-vingt-douze pour cent des gens possèdent un téléphone portable en Europe. Et les SMS sont devenus une partie essentielle de cette révolution numérique. En Angleterre, plus d'un milliard de messages sont envoyés par mois. En France, ce sont
10 35 millions de vœux électroniques qui ont été échangés le premier janvier 2013.

## Qui sont les « texters » ?

Mais qui sont les agités du pouce ? Si tout le monde envoie des messages de temps en temps, les véritables adeptes, qui privilégient ce moyen de communication, sont essentiellement les plus jeunes.
15 90 % des ados préféreraient envoyer des messages que de parler de vive voix au téléphone. Et les jeunes adultes ne sont pas en reste : 78 % des Français de 18–24 ans sont des habitués des SMS. Les

⇨

⇨

femmes seraient un peu plus textos que les hommes, mais on ne
peut guère parler de la féminisation du pouce : les hommes s'en
20  servent chaque jour aussi ! Les utilisations majoritaires seraient les
messages d'amour, l'amitié et autres fonctions plutôt relationnelles
et sociales. Le développement des textos est tel que certains
spécialistes n'hésitent pas à parler d'addiction, et des cliniques
proposent même des cures de désintoxication.

## Un monde à part

25  Mais surtout aujourd'hui les messages textes sont devenus un
moyen à part entière de contacter son réseau de proches. Et cela
s'adresse pratiquement exclusivement au cercle d'amis : une
étude anglaise a montré que les « texters » n'envoient pas des
SMS indifféremment à tout leur carnet d'adresse. Ils envoient de
30  manière intensive des textos à un petit groupe d'amis. Les SMS
sont envoyés moins facilement à un membre de la famille.

À noter que de nouvelles fonctionnalités, telles que l'accès aux
logiciels de messagerie instantanée du web sur son mobile,
devraient renforcer ce phénomène.

## Le pouce des timides

35  Certains spécialistes pensent que les textos sont, encore plus
que les forums de discussions, la bouée de sauvetage des grands
timides et les phobiques sociaux. En clair, tous ceux qui ont du
mal à s'exprimer en face à face. Ces véritables « handicapés
sociaux » en sont réduits à même éviter la conversation
40  téléphonique pour lui préférer le message texte. Des scientifiques
ont montré que les personnes qui ont tendance à nouer des
amitiés plutôt dans le monde virtuel de l'Internet sont aussi plus
attirées par les messages textes. Les SMS seraient même utilisés
par certains à la manière d'un « chat ». Avec l'avantage pour les
45  timides d'avoir plus de temps pour réfléchir à ses réponses.

## Y a klk1 ?

Si le SMS est devenu un mode de communication à part entière, il
a aussi son langage ... qui d'ailleurs **hérisse le poil**\* des puristes.
Écriture phonétique, lettres qui remplacent des syllabes ... Pour les
plus âgés, cela ne ressemble à rien. Celui-ci renforce encore plus
50  le sentiment d'appartenance à un groupe, avec son langage et ses
codes. Mais ses détracteurs soulignent que cette simplification limite
la richesse de la discussion. Il est difficile en effet de philosopher en
langage SMS ... On notera néanmoins des initiatives intéressantes,
telles que les fables de La Fontaine en SMS publiées par Phil Marso.

55  Même si vous êtes un adepte des SMS, n'oubliez pas tout de
même de rencontrer vos amis dans la vraie vie. Et alors éteignez
votre portable !

*Glossary*

hérisser le poil                                                              *annoy*

# Questions ?

This article describes how texting is becoming more used in France.

Re-read lines 6–11.

1 The article gives some information about the growth of texting in Europe. What **three** statistics does it state? **3**

..................................................................................................................................................................

..................................................................................................................................................................

..................................................................................................................................................................

Re-read lines 12–22.

2 The article goes on to discuss who is using texting.
   **a)** Which group of people use texts most? **1**

   ..................................................................................................................................................................

   **b)** What do we learn about the relative use by men and women? **1**

   ..................................................................................................................................................................

   **c)** What are the main reasons for using texts? **2**

   ..................................................................................................................................................................

   ..................................................................................................................................................................

Re-read lines 25–34.

3 The author talks about who is texted.
   **a)** Who are the main recipients of text messages? **1**

   ..................................................................................................................................................................

   **b)** Who is less likely to receive a text? **1**

   ..................................................................................................................................................................

   **c)** What is likely to increase text use in the future? **1**

   ..................................................................................................................................................................

Re-read lines 35–45.

4 We learn more about texters.
   **a)** Who is texting really useful for? **1**

   ..................................................................................................................................................................

   **b)** Why is this the case? State **two** reasons. **2**

   ..................................................................................................................................................................

   ..................................................................................................................................................................

⇨

⇨

Re-read lines 46–58.

5   The author looks at text language.
    **a)** Who has difficulty with text language?  **1**

    .........................................................................................................................................................

    **b)** What advantages and disadvantages does text language have? Give details.  **2**

    .........................................................................................................................................................

    .........................................................................................................................................................

    **c)** What final pieces of advice does the author give?  **2**

    .........................................................................................................................................................

    .........................................................................................................................................................

6   Now consider the article as a whole. Does the author give the impression of being in favour of texting
    or against it? Give details from the text to justify your answer.  **2**

    .........................................................................................................................................................

    .........................................................................................................................................................

Total **20**

7   Now translate lines 1–5 (En quelques années … suffit !).

## Answers

### La vogue des rencontres sur Internet

1  a) From 9 p.m. to midnight/When her children are in bed/Twice a week on Tuesdays and Fridays **3**
   b) Strangers **1**
2  a) To meet new people in order to find a long term partner/**or** to meet lots of people/To break out of loneliness/**or** just to meet new people simply because you can (Any two) **2**
   b) Put single people in contact with each other/Allow them to send messages to each other (communicate) **2**
   c) There are around 12 million people living on their own/One French person in five lives alone/These people are dreaming of evenings with more than the TV for company (Any two) **2**
3  a) He does not agree: it is a phenomenon of society (**or**, a change in the way people on their own behave) **1**
   b) At work, or evenings with friends **2**
4  a) A colleague told her she had met her husband on the internet **1**
   b) (The great) love **1**
5  a) A screen name (ID) that fits your personality **1**
   b) Your personal email address you use for friends and family/Your business (professional) email address **2**
6  She sees it as positive: she talks about how many people use it/She talks about people dreaming of finding someone/It is becoming the main way to meet someone/Patricia's colleague met her partner there/Patricia is positive about it/You are told how to sign up **2**

Total **20**

7  I was coming out very unhappily from a difficult divorce,/sure I would never find happiness./Between my work as a teacher and my two children,/I didn't have time to go out,/never mind to meet new friends.

## Answers

### Scolarité : le redoublement est-il un échec ?

1  a) Every year on average more than 60,000 students repeat a year/1000 parents and teachers were surveyed/65% of parents and 58% of teachers were in favour of it **3**
   b) It can be demotivating **1**
   c) Countries with a high rate of repeating perform less well in education than those with a low rate **1**
2  a) They can start again on a better basis **1**
   b) A first year pupil finding it hard to adapt to secondary school/An adolescent for whom changes to themselves are more important than school **2**
   c) It should not be seen as a punishment **1**
3  a) Discuss it with the school **1**
   b) Guidance counsellors and teachers/work in the students' interests **2**
   c) At parents' nights (meetings between staff and parents) **1**
   d) That parents and children do not always want the same thing **2**
4  a) They suggest students who are having difficulty at this stage follow a different path (technical or professional school) **2**

⇨

➡️

b) Teachers advise, but familes make the final decision **1**

5 They are trying to give a balanced view: often the author asks questions, and gives two different viewpoints/They quote Mme Sultan who is in favour/but refer to students as 'victims'/Some people say it is the best thing, others say it is a waste of time/They quote statistics saying most people are in favour, but balance that with statistics to show it might not be effective/When they talk about not disagreeing with repeating, they make it clear they are quoting a point of view/They never give an opinion of their own **2**

Total **20**

6 Repeating can be an opportunity for a pupil/who has experienced a drama in his or her life/(a death in the family, for instance)/and for the one who is not doing very well in school/but nevertheless is making efforts to get better marks.

## Answers

### La mode du sport : les baskets et les jogging !

1 a) They signed the first non-sporting contract/with Adidas (the sports goods manufacturer)/They sold 22 million dollars' worth of Adidas products the first weekend they were on sale
(Any two) **2**

b) 79% mention sports clothing names when they are thinking about brands **1**

2 a) Young American girls are supposed to wear pink and white sports clothing, worn loose/Young French girls (Parisian girls) like tight jeans and rock clothes **2**

b) They have recruited people to research street trends in Europe/and send the results to HQ/Portland **2**

3 a) Taupe-coloured tops/Tight-fitting leggings **2**

b) Males are more focused on sport/Female customers on fashion and style **2**

c) It started at a round table discussion in 2000/for Adidas and creators to discuss style/Stella was into sport and asked why sports clothing looked awful
(Any two) **2**

4 He may not be the best-looking guy/but he is the coolest/and his girlfriend is the best **3**

5 a) Who will invent the equivalent of the hoodie for the 21st century? **1**

b) Jeans are still seen as casual wear **1**

6 The author is in favour of this style of fashion: he uses words like *cool* and *branché* (up-to-date) very often/He cites names from fashion and music/He discusses how successful Stella McCartney has been/He gives positive reports about what Adidas and Puma are doing/In the last paragraph he looks forward to the future **2**

Total **20**

7 Until now, for sports brands,/all their energy was concentrated on technology and performance./Women, who only represent 30% of their customers, make up *the* market of tomorrow./Before, they took men's clothes, cut them shorter and narrower,/and there you had the feminine line.

## Answers

### SMS, textos : dites « Je t'M » avec le pouce !

1 More than 92% of people in France own a mobile phone/In England more than a billion texts are sent each month/35 million greetings were texted on 1 January 2013 **3**

2 a) The young **1**

 b) Women send texts a bit more than men **1**

 c) Messages of love, friendship/and other functions to do with social relationships **2**

3 a) A circle of friends **1**

 b) A family member **1**

 c) New functions, such as access to the internet **1**

4 a) Shy people (people who are social phobics) **1**

 b) They have trouble communicating face to face/They avoid phone conversations and prefer texts/They like to have time to think about their answers (Any two) **2**

5 a) Older people or purists **1**

 b) Advantages: spelling as it sounds and letters to replace syllables **or** it increases the feeling of belonging to a group

 Disadvantages: it limits the richness of discussion (language) **2**

 c) Don't forget to meet your friends for real and switch off your phone **2**

6 The author gives the impression of being in favour of texting: he talks about how popular and widespread it is/He talks about the positive things it is used for/He does mention the idea of addiction to texts, but then moves on/He talks about how use will continue to grow, without any negative comment/He discusses how texting can be of great value to shy people/He discusses how it simplifies communication/While he says some people see it as limiting, he then goes on to counter that with new developments **2**

Total **20**

7 In a few years, text messages or SMS are now sent by all mobile phone users!/To such an extent that the thumb has become/an organ of communication all by itself./Who would still send a love letter by post on Valentine's Day?/A text message is enough!

# Introduction

Listening is worth **25%** of your final mark. It will take the form of a monologue or presentation, followed by a dialogue, in which one person is asked and answers questions on a topic. You will be asked questions about the interviewee's answers. The assessments will follow the same format as at National 5, but will be at a higher level of difficulty. However, for the National 5 exam, you hear the dialogue three times, and for the Higher exam just twice. The monologue will last up to two minutes, there will be a minute's gap, then you will hear it again. There will be a gap of two minutes, to allow you to complete the questions, then you will have a minute to study the next set of questions. The conversation will last two to three minutes, then you will hear it again after a further minute.

## Remember

☞ Practice is key to doing well in the listening.
☞ Listen to music and watch films/television programmes in French.
☞ Tackling a listening you have already done a few months later is a real support to your listening skills.

When practising for or actually doing the assessment, make sure that the first time through you simply listen, and are not tempted to jot down notes, as that may make you miss important information that is following. Just listen and make mental notes as to where you have to concentrate particularly hard the next time. If you can get into this habit, it will help you do the same in the final exam. Many people feel they will have forgotten the answers by the time they come to write them down, but trust your own memory!

The skill of note-taking is very important: you are not allowed a dictionary for the listening exam, so it makes sense to write your notes in English, but sometimes it could be useful to write down a word you are not sure of in French, to think about once the recording is no longer being played.

Listen extra carefully for details you are required to give in your answer. Just as at National 5, if you are not sure of an answer, do not be afraid to guess, as you will get no marks for a blank, but may for an intelligent guess. Equally, as at National 5, if the answer asks for two things, just give two things! The examiner will only give you marks for two things you write down, and so writing more is a waste of time. The only time it might make sense to write more will be if you are not sure which bits of what you have heard are actually the answer wanted.

So what do you do when you are sitting the exam? What is the best way to go about it? Here are some steps to take that should help you do your best.

## Hints & tips ⭐

- ✓ When you are told to open your paper, do so and read the information at the start, which sets the scene.
- ✓ Draw a line towards the left of the page, and put your notes in this left margin when it is time (you should transfer your final answers to the right of the line at the end, and score out your notes with a single line).
- ✓ Read all the questions carefully, as this will prepare you for what the dialogue is about.
- ✓ Look for question words, such as **why** and **when**, in order to know what information you are looking for.
- ✓ Make sure you get the basics such as numbers, times, dates and all the vocabulary for places, weather, and so on (you will find these in the structures and vocabulary chapter, Chapter 12, to revise from).
- ✓ Keep your concentration going for the whole time, and do not try to write out your final answers before the last playing of the CD or soundfile has finished.

How can you get better at listening? The answer is practice. Try using any listening material you can get hold of, such as Scholar Higher listenings. Watch video clips online in French, to hear French spoken. Watch films in French, with the subtitles showing in French, to help you follow what is going on. When you have done a listening assessment or task, listen to it again, but with the script in front of you, to help you associate the heard word with the written one.

The topic of the listening will be drawn from the contexts you have studied over the course of the year. The list below shows all the topic areas that make up a possible Higher Course. However, do not worry if you think you have not covered everything here, as the listening will not be based on an area that many people will not have covered in depth.

# Contexts and topics of Higher

| Society | Family and friends | Becoming an adult/new family structure/marriage/partnership/ gang culture/bullying/social influences and pressures |
|---|---|---|
| | Lifestyle | Teenage problems, e.g. smoking, drugs, alcohol |
| | Media | Impact of the digital age |
| | Global languages | Minority languages and their importance/association with culture |
| | Citizenship | Global citizenship/democracy/politics/power |
| Learning | Learning in context | Understanding self as a learner, e.g. learning styles/importance of language learning |
| | Education | Advantages/disadvantages of higher or further education, choosing a university/college, lifelong learning |
| Employability | Jobs | Getting a summer job, planning for future jobs/higher education, gap year, career path, equality in the workplace |
| | Work and CVs | Preparing for a job interview/importance of language in global contexts, job opportunities |
| Culture | Planning a trip | Taking a gap year/working abroad (mobility)/travel |
| | Other countries | Living in a multicultural society/stereotypes/prejudice and racism |
| | Celebrating a special event | Social influences on/importance of traditions, customs and beliefs in another country |
| | Literature of another country | Literature – analysis and evaluation |
| | Film and television | Studying the media of another country |

# Introduction

The monologues and dialogues on the website (www.hoddergibson.co.uk; click on 'Updates and Extras') are played twice, with a gap of one minute in between each reading. Try and stick to this, to give you more practice for the real exams. For a monologue, including the two listenings, you should complete the task in 10 minutes. For the dialogue, give yourself 20 minutes for your answers.

The monologues and dialogues are based on the four contexts of Higher French, but each one may well cover more than one topic area.

# Monologue 1
## Society, problems

🔊 *In France, you hear a radio report about young people and drug taking, la toxicomanie.*

## Questions ❓

1  How does the speaker describe adolescence?  **1**

.......................................................................................................

2  Why do young people sometimes see taking drugs as positive?  **1**

.......................................................................................................

3  We hear a number of reasons for young people taking up drugs: state any **two** of them.  **2**

.......................................................................................................

.......................................................................................................

4  Which kind of drug user is more common?  **1**

.......................................................................................................

5  What does the speaker say has happened when young people become addicted? Give details.  **2**

.......................................................................................................

.......................................................................................................

6  The speaker names some people who might support young people: state any one of them.  **1**

.......................................................................................................

# Dialogue 1
## Society, problems

🔊 *Francine talks about young people and their attitude to drinking alcohol in France.*

## Questions ❓

1 Does she think young French people drink like young Scottish and English people? **1**

...................................................................................................................................................

2 How have things changed in French families at mealtimes? **2**

...................................................................................................................................................

...................................................................................................................................................

3 When do young French people drink now? **2**

...................................................................................................................................................

...................................................................................................................................................

4 What has changed for young French people? Give details. **2**

...................................................................................................................................................

...................................................................................................................................................

5 Why do young people not always go to cafés to meet their friends? **1**

...................................................................................................................................................

6 Is the situation the same for boys and girls? Explain your answer. **2**

...................................................................................................................................................

...................................................................................................................................................

7 What horrifies her about drinking habits in Britain? **2**

...................................................................................................................................................

...................................................................................................................................................

# Monologue 2
## Society, family structures

🔊 *You hear this report about changes to family structures in France including 'PACS', civil partnerships.*

### Questions ❓

1 What has changed about the number of marriages over the last 100 years? **1**

.........................................................................................................................................

2 What does the report define 'PACS' as? **1**

.........................................................................................................................................

3 Why is 'PACS' considered revolutionary? **1**

.........................................................................................................................................

4 How many marriages in France end in separation and divorce? **1**

.........................................................................................................................................

5 What other fact does the report state about the rise in divorce? **1**

.........................................................................................................................................

6 The speaker gives several pieces of information about single-parent families. State any **two**. **2**

.........................................................................................................................................

.........................................................................................................................................

7 The speaker gives details about contact between fathers and their children. State one statistic she gives. **1**

.........................................................................................................................................

# Dialogue 2
## Society, family structures

🔊 *Sylvain talks about how he gets on with the other members of his family.*

## Questions ❓

1  What does Sylvain tell you about his family? State any **two** things.  **2**

..................................................................................................................................

..................................................................................................................................

2  Why does his father not live with him?  **2**

..................................................................................................................................

..................................................................................................................................

3  How does he feel about it?  **1**

..................................................................................................................................

4  When does he see his father? Give details.  **2**

..................................................................................................................................

..................................................................................................................................

5  Why are things arranged the way they are?  **2**

..................................................................................................................................

..................................................................................................................................

6  When does he see the grandparents who live further away?  **1**

..................................................................................................................................

7  What does he tell you about his sister? State any **two** things.  **2**

..................................................................................................................................

..................................................................................................................................

# Monologue 3
## Learning, language learning

🔊 *You hear this report about the teaching of languages in French schools.*

### Questions ❓

1 Who has launched a new plan? **1**

...................................................................................................................................................

2 How many foreign languages should French students learn now? **1**

...................................................................................................................................................

3 Where is the emphasis in primary and early secondary education? **1**

...................................................................................................................................................

4 What should students be able to do by the end of primary school? **2**

...................................................................................................................................................

...................................................................................................................................................

5 What kind of situation should students at the end of lower secondary be able to get by in? **1**

...................................................................................................................................................

6 What should a student at the end of their time at *lycée* be able to understand? **1**

...................................................................................................................................................

7 What should students be able to do with a news item? State one thing. **1**

...................................................................................................................................................

# Dialogue 3
## Learning, language learning

🔊 *Marie-Claire talks about learning languages at school.*

### Questions ❓

1  What does Marie-Claire say when asked if she liked school? State **two** things.  **2**

.................................................................................................................................

.................................................................................................................................

2  What was good about her first school? State any **two** things.  **2**

.................................................................................................................................

.................................................................................................................................

3  What does she say about her German and English teachers? Give details.  **2**

.................................................................................................................................

.................................................................................................................................

4  What was her problem with her second school? State any **two** things.  **2**

.................................................................................................................................

.................................................................................................................................

5  What else did she not like? State one thing.  **1**

.................................................................................................................................

6  What was good about her second school? State **two** things.  **2**

.................................................................................................................................

.................................................................................................................................

7  What was the best thing for her about the second school?  **1**

.................................................................................................................................

# Monologue 4
## Employability, careers

🔊 *You listen to a radio programme, where a girl who is training as a food technician has asked about how to start work.*

**Questions** ❓

1 What **two** things does the speaker say the girl might not have? **2**

......................................................................................................................................

......................................................................................................................................

2 What does she think the girl should consider doing? **1**

......................................................................................................................................

3 Why would this be important for her? **1**

......................................................................................................................................

4 What would be the ideal thing for the girl? **1**

......................................................................................................................................

5 What other possibilities are there for her? State **two** possibilities. **2**

......................................................................................................................................

......................................................................................................................................

6 Why is it important to make sure you take part in a work placement? **1**

......................................................................................................................................

# Dialogue 4
## Employability, careers

🔊 *Yvonne is being interviewed about her plans for the future.*

## Questions ❓

1 Where does Yvonne work part-time? Why does she work there? **2**

.......................................................................................................................................

.......................................................................................................................................

2 Give details about where she comes from. **2**

.......................................................................................................................................

.......................................................................................................................................

3 What does she tell you about her future plans? **2**

.......................................................................................................................................

.......................................................................................................................................

4 She discusses problems she has with her students in Scotland. State one of them. **1**

.......................................................................................................................................

5 Why might she stay on in Scotland? **1**

.......................................................................................................................................

6 Why does she think it would be possible for her to settle in Scotland? State **two** things. **2**

.......................................................................................................................................

.......................................................................................................................................

7 What do both of her parents think of this possibility? **2**

.......................................................................................................................................

.......................................................................................................................................

# Monologue 5
## Employability, working

🔊 *You hear a radio programme giving advice to students on holiday jobs.*

## Questions ?

1 What **two** times are suitable for students to find jobs? **2**

.......................................................................................................................................................

.......................................................................................................................................................

2 What might the work help the students do? State one thing. **1**

.......................................................................................................................................................

3 Why might a student have to work? **1**

.......................................................................................................................................................

4 Where do employers look for holiday cover? **1**

.......................................................................................................................................................

5 What kind of employment is possible in certain regions? **1**

.......................................................................................................................................................

6 Where else might you look for a temporary job? **1**

.......................................................................................................................................................

7 Why might students find getting a holiday job difficult? State any one reason. **1**

.......................................................................................................................................................

# Dialogue 5
## Employability, working

🔊 *Yvonne talks about her part-time job.*

**Questions** ❓

1 What does she tell you about her job? Give **two** details. **2**

..................................................................................................................

..................................................................................................................

2 What are the **two** reasons that she says she has to work? **2**

..................................................................................................................

..................................................................................................................

3 How does she feel about her part-time job? State **two** things. **2**

..................................................................................................................

..................................................................................................................

4 When does she find problems with her work? Why? **2**

..................................................................................................................

..................................................................................................................

5 Why did she not have a part-time job when she was a student in France? **1**

..................................................................................................................

6 She did work in France. When was this, and what did she do? **2**

..................................................................................................................

..................................................................................................................

7 What did she like most about this job? **1**

..................................................................................................................

# Monologue 6
## Culture, working abroad

🔊 *You hear a podcast about French people who choose to live and work abroad.*

**1** How many French people have gone abroad to work in the last ten years? **1**

..................................................................................................................................................

**2** What **two** things encourage young French graduates to work abroad? **2**

..................................................................................................................................................

..................................................................................................................................................

**3** What do some professionals hope for? **1**

..................................................................................................................................................

**4** What does the speaker say is not enough when considering working abroad? **1**

..................................................................................................................................................

**5** One employee later regretted his situation. Why had he wanted to go abroad? **1**

..................................................................................................................................................

**6** What was the problem with his attempt? **1**

..................................................................................................................................................

**7** What was the final result for him? **1**

..................................................................................................................................................

# Dialogue 6
## Culture, working abroad

🔊 *Vincent talks about the differences between eating in France and in Scotland.*

## Questions ❓

1  What is the main difference Vincent notices about where he is?  **1**

.....................................................................................................

2  What does he tell us about breakfast in France and Scotland?  **2**

.....................................................................................................

.....................................................................................................

3  What does he feel about 'a full English breakfast'?  **1**

.....................................................................................................

4  What does he say about lunch and Scotland? Give **two** details.  **2**

.....................................................................................................

.....................................................................................................

5  Why does he mention school students? State **two** things.  **2**

.....................................................................................................

.....................................................................................................

6  What does he tell you about his own habits in France when at school?  **1**

.....................................................................................................

7  What does he do at lunchtime in Scotland?  **1**

.....................................................................................................

8  What is for him the main difference in restaurants in the two countries?  **2**

.....................................................................................................

.....................................................................................................

# Monologue 7

## Culture, travel

🔊 *You hear this report about holiday planning.*

### Questions ❓

1 What should you do to make your journey stress free? **1**

.............................................................................................................................................................

2 What else should you do in preparation? Why? **2**

.............................................................................................................................................................

.............................................................................................................................................................

3 The speaker mentions several downsides of the sun. State one of them. **1**

.............................................................................................................................................................

4 What does the speaker say you should not trust? **1**

.............................................................................................................................................................

5 What might turn a holiday into tragedy? **1**

.............................................................................................................................................................

6 What might you do to avert this? State one thing. **1**

.............................................................................................................................................................

7 What should you never do, according to the final piece of advice? **1**

.............................................................................................................................................................

# Dialogue 7
## Culture, travel

🔊 *Jacques talks about his experiences of holidays with his family and his friends.*

## Questions ?

1 How old was Jacques on his first holiday away from his parents? **1**

.................................................................................................................

2 Who was his first independent holiday with? **1**

.................................................................................................................

3 Where did he go, and what did he do there? **2**

.................................................................................................................

.................................................................................................................

4 Why did he like this holiday? Give any **two** reasons. **2**

.................................................................................................................

.................................................................................................................

5 What annoyed him about going on holiday with his parents? State **two** things. **2**

.................................................................................................................

.................................................................................................................

6 Where does he go on holiday with his girlfriend nowadays? **1**

.................................................................................................................

7 What method of travel do they use? **1**

.................................................................................................................

8 What does he enjoy doing on holiday now? State any **two** details. **2**

.................................................................................................................

.................................................................................................................

# Monologue 1
## Society, problems

### Answers

1 A period of new experiments **1**
2 The risk attached to taking drugs/**or** the attraction of something forbidden **1**
3 Feeling abandoned after parents' divorce/ Difficulty in finding a meaning in life/Wanting to belong to a group/Reduce tensions (Any two) **2**
4 The occasional user/Someone who takes drugs from time to time **1**
5 Has passed beyond rebellion/Is at odds with the family background/Is in with people who find drugs important (Any two) **2**
6 psychiatrists/psychologists/specialists in prevention (Any one) **1**

# Dialogue 1
## Society, problems

### Answers

1 No **1**
2 Children used to drink a little wine with water at mealtimes/Now it is water or fruit juice **2**
3 Family parties/Special occasions like birthdays or weddings **2**
4 They used to have to stay home after 6 or 6.30/Now they can go out in the evening **2**
5 It is expensive/It is not very private (Either one) **1**
6 No, girls do not have so much freedom/ They have to be home earlier/They are better at doing homework (Any two) **2**
7 Very young people (12 or 13) drunk/ Drinking not only beer but also vodka/ Sometimes you find them unconscious in the streets (Any two) **2**

# Monologue 2
## Society, family structures

**Answers**

1 Dropped from 600,000 a year to 200,000 **1**
2 Civil union or contract between two people (to organise their life) **1**
3 It allows gay partnerships **1**
4 One in three **1**
5 People are divorcing earlier/sooner/**or** marriages are not lasting as long **1**

6 One person is in charge of the children/ It is usually the mother/after a divorce or separation/25% of families in France are single-parent families (Any two) **2**
7 Many children only see their father once a fortnight. One in four never see their father. (Any one) **1**

# Dialogue 2
## Society, family structures

**Answers**

1 Lives with his mum and sister/Grandparents live next door/Uncle, aunt and cousins live 30 metres away/Dad in the next village (Any two) **2**
2 It was not working/Parents were always fighting/Nobody was happy **2**
3 Would prefer if his dad was with them but accepts it **1**

4 After school (to do his homework)/The weekend to do things **2**
5 His dad is a teacher and can help with homework/His mum works late **2**
6 Summer holidays and Christmas **1**
7 She is young (11)/She is very funny/They don't argue/She often goes to their cousins' (Any two) **2**

# Monologue 3
## Learning, language learning

**Answers**

1 Education ministry **1**
2 Two **1**
3 Oral work **1**
4 Communicate simply (if their partner speaks slowly and clearly)/Exchange (simple) information **2**

5 Where they meet problems when travelling **1**
6 Essential information in a complex text **1**
7 Give an opinion on it/ Discuss or debate it (Any one) **1**

# Dialogue 3
## Learning, language learning

### Answers

1 Liked her first school/Thought her second school was awful **2**
2 Near her house/could have lunch at home/ Knew everyone in her class (Any two) **2**
3 Her German teacher was very sarcastic (looking for mistakes when they spoke)/ English teacher encouraged them to always speak English in class **2**
4 She had to take the train there/It was 20 kilometres away/She left home at 6.30 a.m. and got home at 7 p.m. (Any two) **2**

5 Her friends had gone to other schools/She felt isolated (lonely)/She didn't meet her classmates after school (Any one) **1**
6 She was in a European (bilingual) class/She did some subjects (history) in English)/She found it important to speak English well (Any two) **2**
7 She got good results **1**

# Monologue 4
## Employability, careers

### Answers

1 Professional experience/Not yet got her qualification (diploma) **2**
2 Get a part-time job **1**
3 Without experience it will be hard to get a job when she is finished **1**
4 Finding a company that would employ her at the end, if they liked her **1**

5 Working in a market/Job in a supermarket/ a fast food place **2**
6 Without experience you risk not finding a job **1**

# Dialogue 4

## Employability, careers

### Answers

1 She works in a bar/To get to know people **2**
2 A village in the north of France/Half an hour (30 km) from Lille **2**
3 She will go home to finish her studies/Then come back to Scotland to become a teacher **2**
4 Some of them refuse to speak in class/Others ask why they have to learn French (Either one) **1**
5 Her boyfriend is there **1**
6 Glasgow is not unlike Lille/Flights home are not expensive **2**
7 Her mother would prefer her to stay in France/Her father is happy (because he loves golf and can play whenever he comes) **2**

# Monologue 5

## Employability, working

### Answers

1 Winter holidays/Summer holidays **2**
2 Spend money in the sales/Pay towards their studying (Either one) **1**
3 Not all parents can afford to support them **1**
4 Job agencies **1**
5 Agricultural (picking fruit and vegetables) **1**
6 Café or restaurant **1**
7 These jobs are in demand/There are limited offers/There are a lot of other people looking for holiday jobs (Any one) **1**

# Dialogue 5

## Employability, working

### Answers

1 She works in a bar/Thursdays from 8 till 12/8 hours on Saturdays (Any two) **2**
2 She is an assistant in a school/and her flat is expensive **2**
3 It is well paid/She gets to meet people **2**
4 On Fridays/She is tired when she has to go to school **2**
5 She stayed at home/didn't have to pay for rent and food (Either one) **1**
6 In the summer holidays/(An assistant) in a holiday camp **2**
7 Seeing the children enjoy themselves **1**

# Monologue 6
## Culture, working abroad

### Answers

1 Nearly 600,000  **1**
2 Fed up of unemployment/Looking for more interesting careers  **2**
3 Things being better (the best)  **1**
4 A spirit of adventure  **1**
5 He thought he was being exploited in his job at the time/**or** He dreamt of leaving  **1**

6 He couldn't find any interesting work/ He was not prepared enough (Either one)  **1**
7 He returned home (disappointed)  **1**

# Dialogue 6
## Culture, working abroad

### Answers

1 The weather/It is colder and rains more (Either one)  **1**
2 France: coffee or hot chocolate with bread (and cereal)/Scotland: hamburger or sausages, eggs and ham (bacon)  **2**
3 Couldn't eat it/he would hate it  **1**
4 Most people keep working and have a drink and a sandwich/Others go jogging and eat something quickly  **2**
5 They eat sandwiches or chips in the street/They don't sit down  **2**

6 He went home for a meal made by his mother  **1**
7 He takes an hour/eats a main course and pudding  **1**
8 Most French restaurants offer French food/Hardly any restaurants in Scotland have Scottish food **or** Curry seems to be the main Scottish dish  **2**

# Monologue 7
## Culture, travel

**Answers**

1 Plan and organise it **1**
2 Get fit by doing exercise (any examples)/
Your health is at risk otherwise **2**
3 Increases lines/Makes your skin older/Can
give you skin cancer
(Any one) **1**

4 Sun cream **1**
5 Drowning/accidents at the beach **1**
6 Be careful/Obey safety advice/Respect the flags
(Any one) **1**
7 Never swim alone **1**

# Dialogue 7
## Culture, travel

**Answers**

1 13 **1**
2 His friends **1**
3 Brittany/Camping and cycling **or** Spent a
week in Saint Malo **2**
4 They got up late/They didn't have to see
monuments (sights)/They ate when and
what they wanted
(Any two) **2**

5 Had to get up at 8 for breakfast/Had to
be back at 1 for lunch **2**
6 Greece or Spain **1**
7 Plane **1**
8 (New) sports/Sub-aqua (diving) **or**
Windsurfing **2**

## Monologue 1
### Society, problems

*In France, you hear a radio report about young people, drug-taking and drug addiction, la toxicomanie.*

L'adolescence est une période d'expérimentations nouvelles. Ces expérimentations encouragent des jeunes à prendre des risques. Pour certains jeunes il y a l'attraction négative. C'est-à-dire, le risque et les conséquences graves qui sont attachés à la consommation de la drogue. Pour d'autres jeunes c'est l'attraction aux choses interdites.

**Hints & tips** ⭐

✓ *Once you have completed a listening and used the marking scheme to mark it, listen to it again with the transcript in front of you. This will help you to develop an ear for French.*

✓ *Use the transcripts as a source for material to use in your own writing and talking.*

Deux causes principales expliquent en partie la consommation de drogue par l'adolescent : le sentiment d'abandon après le divorce des parents ; la difficulté de trouver un sens à la vie en général. Vouloir s'intégrer à un groupe, réduire les tensions, sont également pourquoi l'adolescent commence à se droguer.

Il faut distinguer entre les jeunes qui se droguent de temps en temps et ceux qui se droguent régulièrement. Le premier est le plus fréquent et donc ne doit pas trop inquiéter. Ils le font tout simplement pour montrer qu'ils sont indépendants et peuvent faire ce qu'ils veulent. Ils veulent qu'on les traite comme des adultes.

Par contre ceux qui se droguent régulièrement ne sont plus des rebelles, mais ils sont devenus des toxicomanes. Ce type d'adolescent perd le contact avec son milieu familial et fréquente souvent des milieux où la consommation de drogue est importante. Pour ces jeunes il faut l'aide des psychiatres et des psychologues qui sont des spécialistes dans le monde de la prévention et de la médicalisation de la drogue.

# Dialogue 1
## Society, problems

*Francine talks about young people and their attitude to drinking alcohol in France.*

**Question :** Francine, j'ai entendu que les jeunes en France ont commencé à boire de l'alcool comme les britanniques : est-ce que vous avez remarqué cela vous-même ?

**Francine :** Il ne faut pas exagérer ! Rien en France ressemble aux rues d'une grande ville en Angleterre ou en Écosse le samedi soir. Mais bien sûr, les jeunes ont tendance à boire entre eux maintenant plus qu'avant.

**Question :** Est-ce qu'on a encore l'habitude comme dans les autres générations d'apprendre à boire en famille ?

**Francine :** Je crois moins : autrefois les petits enfants prenaient un verre de vin mixé avec de l'eau à table le soir, mais maintenant on est plus conscient de la santé des enfants, et on leur offre du jus de fruit ou de l'eau à table.

**Question :** Alors les jeunes Français ne boivent plus du vin à table ?

**Francine :** Mais si, mais surtout à des fêtes de famille, ou pour les occasions exceptionnelles, comme les anniversaires, les mariages, des choses comme ça. Et même là, on commence plus tard, les enfants sont plus âgés, ils ont au moins douze/treize ans maintenant.

**Question :** Vous avez dit que les jeunes boivent entre eux : qu'est-ce que ça veut dire ?

**Francine :** Autrefois les jeunes avaient moins de liberté, ils devaient rester à la maison le soir après six heures, six heures et demie du soir. Maintenant ils peuvent sortir le soir : c'est là qu'ils s'achètent des bières pour boire ensemble.

**Question :** Ils ne vont pas au café ?

**Francine :** Pas forcément : les cafés, ça coûte assez cher et puis ce n'est pas très privé, les jeunes ne peuvent pas être entre eux. Donc on va au supermarché, on achète quelques canettes de bière, et on va au parc.

**Question :** C'est vrai pour les filles comme pour les garçons ?

**Francine :** Dans une certaine mesure : les filles n'ont pas encore autant de liberté que les garçons, elles doivent rentrer plus tôt, puis elles font mieux leurs devoirs que les garçons, mais si, on voit aussi des fois des filles dans les parcs !

$\Rightarrow$

⇨

**Question :** Mais ce n'est pas comme ici en Grande Bretagne ?

**Francine :** Ah non, ici on voit les jeunes totalement ivres, beaucoup plus jeunes qu'en France, les jeunes quelquefois de douze/treize ans, et en plus ils ne boivent pas de la bière, ils boivent de la vodka, des boissons fortement alcoolisées. On les trouve inconscients dans les rues, quelquefois.

# Monologue 2
## Society, family structures

*You hear this report about changes to family structures in France over the last hundred years.*

Depuis les années 20, le nombre de mariages est passé d'environ 600 milles mariages par an à 200 milles. L'âge du premier mariage aussi a augmenté. Il est passée d'environ 24 ans à 28 ans. Une alternative ? Il existe aussi une alternative, le PACS (Pacte Civil de Solidarité), une sorte d'union civile. C'est un contrat entre deux personnes (les partenaires), qui leur permet d'organiser leur vie commune. Cette alternative au mariage est en quelque sorte « révolutionnaire », car elle autorise l'union de personnes homosexuelles.

Le taux de divorce augmente chaque année et les chiffres sont là pour le prouver : en France, un mariage sur trois se termine par une séparation. En plus ces divorces interviennent de plus en plus tôt, parce que les mariages durent de moins en moins longtemps.

Une famille monoparentale est une famille constituée d'un seul adulte et d'au moins un enfant, alors des familles où un seul parent a la charge des enfants. Le plus souvent c'est la mère (après un divorce ou une séparation). Le gouvernement a estimé que 25 % des familles sont monoparentales, et, que beaucoup d'enfants séparés voient leur père tous les 15 jours, un enfant sur quatre pas du tout.

# Dialogue 2
## Society, family structures

*Sylvain talks about how he gets on with the other members of his family.*

**Question :** Sylvain, vous avez une grande famille ?

**Sylvain :** Alors, oui et non. J'habite chez ma mère et ma sœur dans un petit village, mais mes grands-parents habitent à côté, mon oncle, ma tante et mes cousines à trente mètres, et mon père dans le prochain village.

**Question :** Vous l'aimez comme ça ?

**Sylvain :** Eh bien, j'aurais préféré que mon père habite encore chez nous, mais ça ne marchait plus, mes parents se bagarraient tout le temps, et personne n'était heureux. Donc il y a quatre ans il a trouvé une nouvelle maison et voilà. Je l'accepte.

**Question :** Vous le voyez souvent ?

**Sylvain :** Ah oui, normalement j'y vais après l'école et je fais mes devoirs là. Je rentre pour dîner. Le weekend on sort souvent ensemble : ou on fait du bowling, ou on va au cinéma le soir.

**Question :** Vous seulement ?

**Sylvain :** Ah non, ma sœur Marie vient aussi : mon père est professeur, donc il peut aider avec les devoirs, et ma mère doit travailler plus tard, donc c'est très convenable pour tout le monde.

**Question :** Et comment vous vous entendez avec vos grands-parents ?

**Sylvain :** Les grands-parents qui habitent à côté de nous, ce sont les parents de ma mère, et on se voit beaucoup. Je les aime bien, mais ils sont assez sévères, donc je préfère aller chez mon père. Mes autres grands-parents je les vois rarement, car ils habitent loin de chez nous, mais on leur rend visite à Noël et pendant les grandes vacances. C'est super chez eux, et ils ne sont pas du tout sévères, on s'amuse très bien là.

**Question :** Vous vous entendez, vous et votre sœur ?

**Sylvain :** Ah oui : elle est assez jeune, elle a onze ans, mais elle est très rigolote, et on ne se dispute jamais. Elle est aussi souvent chez nos cousins.

# Monologue 3
## Learning, language learning

*You hear this report about the teaching of languages in French schools.*

Le ministère de l'Éducation nationale a lancé un plan de rénovation de l'enseignement des langues vivantes étrangères qui concerne tous les élèves de l'école élémentaire au lycée. L'objectif de ce plan est d'améliorer le niveau des élèves dans deux langues étrangères.

Les nouveaux programmes de langues vivantes étrangères à l'école primaire et au collège trouvent l'oral plus important au cours de leur éducation. De nombreuses initiatives ont été lancées pour renforcer l'exposition des élèves à la langue.

À la fin de l'enseignement primaire les élèves doivent communiquer de façon simple si l'interlocuteur parle lentement et distinctement. Ils peuvent aussi échanger des informations simples sur des sujets familiers et habituels.

À la fin du collège les élèves doivent se débrouiller dans la plupart des situations rencontrées en voyage, raconter un événement, une expérience, et défendre une idée.

À la fin du lycée un élève doit comprendre l'essentiel d'un sujet concret ou abstrait dans un texte complexe, et participer dans une discussion technique dans sa spécialité avec un degré de spontanéité et d'aisance. Il peut donner un avis sur un sujet d'actualité et en débattre.

# Dialogue 3
## Learning, language learning
*Marie-Claire talks about learning languages at school.*

**Question :**     Marie-Claire, est-ce que vous aimiez vos jours aller à l'école ?

**Marie-Claire :**     Alors là, j'ai deux réponses : mon collège, je l'aimais bien, mais lorsque je suis allée au lycée à l'âge de quinze ans, j'ai trouvé ça affreux, et je n'étais pas du tout contente de devoir y aller.

**Question :**     Pourquoi aimiez-vous votre collège ?

**Marie-Claire :**     Eh bien, c'était tout près de la maison : nous habitions à cinq cent mètres du collège, donc je pouvais rentrer à midi pour déjeuner chez moi, et je connaissais très bien tout le monde dans ma classe.

**Question :**     Vous aimiez aussi les professeurs ?

**Marie-Claire :**     Oui, ils étaient presque tous gentils, à part ma prof d'allemand : elle était très sarcastique, et aimait trouver les fautes quand on parlait en classe. Mais mon prof d'anglais était complètement différent : il nous encourageait tous à parler en anglais tout le temps en classe.

**Question :**     Et pourquoi le lycée était-il une expérience moins positive ?

**Marie-Claire :**     Ben, d'abord je devais prendre le train pour y aller, car c'était à vingt kilomètres de chez moi, ce qui voulait dire que je devais quitter la maison à six heures et demie, manger à la cantine, puis je ne rentrais le soir qu'à dix-neuf heures, et il me restait des devoirs à faire.

**Question :**     Mais à part ça ?

**Marie-Claire :**     Presque tous mes copains sont allés dans un autre lycée, donc je me sentais assez isolée, car je voyageais seule le matin, et je ne rencontrais pas les autres lycéens après les cours.

**Question :**     Mais vous êtes quand même restée là-bas ?

**Marie-Claire :**     Eh bien je voulais le faire, parce que j'étais dans une classe Européenne ou bilingue, on faisait quelques matières en anglais comme par exemple l'histoire, et puis ça j'appréciais beaucoup, parce que je trouvais ça important de bien parler anglais.    ⇨

⇒

**Question :**     C'était un bon lycée ?

**Marie-Claire :**     Ah oui, bien sûr, et les profs étaient intéressants, et puis j'ai beaucoup appris, et le plus important c'est que j'ai obtenu un bon bac, j'avais de bonnes notes : le problème était plutôt la distance et tout ce que cela voulait dire pour moi.

# Monologue 4
## Employability, careers

*You listen to a radio programme, where a girl who is training as a food technician has asked about how to start work.*

Comment commencer dans le monde du travail ?

Si vous avez une formation de technicien de contrôle de qualité alimentaire, mais n'avez aucune autre expérience professionnelle et n'avez pas encore reçu votre diplôme, vous pourriez penser à faire un boulot à temps partiel. Quel type de boulot pouvez-vous faire ?

Pour vous lancer dans ce domaine, on vous conseille de chercher soit un contrat à temps partiel, soit un stage, dans une société liée au contrôle qualité alimentaire. C'est important car une expérience vous sera nécessaire à la fin de votre formation pour obtenir un poste permanent, c'est-à-dire un contrat de travail, parce que les entreprises n'embauchent pas les personnes sans expérience maintenant.

Idéalement vous pouvez trouver du travail chez une société qui vous promet un contrat à la fin, s'ils sont contents de vous.

Vous pouvez aussi travailler sur un marché. Là, on recrute en permanence et vous restez comme ça dans l'alimentaire. Bien sûr il y a aussi les petits boulots en hypermarchés, McDonald et compagnie, mais essayez de trouver quelque chose, car sinon, à la fin de vos études vous allez vous retrouver dans une situation difficile et risquez de ne pas trouver de boulot dans votre domaine sans avoir d'expérience.

# Dialogue 4
## Employability, careers

*Yvonne is being interviewed about her plans for the future.*

**Question :** Yvonne, vous travaillez à présent à Glasgow : qu'est-ce que vous faites exactement ?

**Yvonne :** D'abord, je suis venue ici pour un an comme assistante dans une école à Glasgow, et ensuite j'ai pris un poste comme serveuse dans un bar, afin de pouvoir rencontrer d'autres jeunes gens.

**Question :** Vous êtes d'où en France ?

**Yvonne :** Je suis étudiante en fac à Lille, mais je suis originaire d'un petit village dans le Nord, Marchiennes, tout près de Lille, pour préciser à trente kilomètres, ou une demi-heure dans le train.

**Question :** Vous comptez retourner en France bientôt ?

**Yvonne :** Oui, bien sûr : je veux reprendre mes études en septembre, et ensuite je resterai encore deux ans pour les finir, mais après j'ai l'intention de revenir en Écosse avec l'intention de devenir professeur.

**Question :** Alors vous aimez les enfants en Écosse, évidemment ceux dans votre école ?

**Yvonne :** Ah oui, la plupart oui : il y en a qui m'offrent des problèmes de temps en temps, alors ils refusent de parler dans la classe et bien sûr il y a ceux qui me demandent tout le temps « Pourquoi est-ce que je dois apprendre le français ? », mais j'ai beaucoup d'élèves qui s'intéressent à la France, et voudraient y aller.

**Question :** Est-ce que vous comptez rester longtemps en Écosse, dès votre retour ici ?

**Yvonne :** Là, je ne sais pas : ça dépend de comment ça se déroulera avec mon petit ami. J'ai rencontré quelqu'un ici, et si ça continue, je veux bien rester longtemps.

**Question :** Vous pourriez imaginer de créer une famille ici ?

**Yvonne :** Oui, bien sûr. Vous savez, Glasgow n'est pas tellement différent de Lille, et puis il y a des vols de l'Écosse à Lille ou la Belgique qui ne sont pas du tout chers, donc comme ça je pourrais rester en contact avec ma famille.

**Question :** Qu'est-ce qu'en pensent vos parents ? $\Rightarrow$

**Yvonne :** Alors, pour ma mère, naturellement elle préférerait que je reste en France, plus proche d'elle, mais elle accepte mes désirs, et mon père est fanatique de golf, donc pour lui, il est content, car comme ça il peut venir n'importe quand faire un petit tour de golf !

# Monologue 5
## Employability, working
*You hear a radio programme giving advice to students on holiday jobs.*

Pour les étudiants, les vacances sont souvent l'occasion de petits boulots pour gagner un peu d'argent. Grandes vacances, vacances d'hiver, c'est le moment pour les jeunes de trouver un boulot de quelques semaines ou quelques jours pour pouvoir ensuite dépenser de l'argent aux soldes, ou tout simplement payer les études. Mais les boulots d'étudiants ne sont pas si faciles à trouver.

La vie d'étudiant n'est pas toujours facile, elle a un coût que malheureusement tous les parents ne peuvent pas supporter, alors l'étudiant doit gagner lui aussi de l'argent. Pour les grandes vacances, les entreprises recherchent parfois des remplaçants pour les vacances, et passent souvent par les sociétés de travail temporaire ; pensez à vous inscrire chez ces agences, pour trouver plus facilement du travail.

Pour les régions productrices de fruits et légumes, il est aussi possible d'approcher des agriculteurs pour du travail physique de ramassage ou d'emballage. Les restaurants ou cafés recrutent parfois aussi durant l'été, des périodes où leur activité explose, donc il existe l'occasion de trouver un contrat de travail durant les grandes vacances. Les étudiants qui désirent travailler peuvent également trouver plusieurs ressources intéressantes sur le net. Les boulots d'étudiants sont très recherchés, pour participer aux frais d'études, se payer le permis de conduire, une voiture, ou s'offrir quelques

⇨

vacances. Les offres d'emploi pourtant sont limitées, et le travail proposé est parfois difficile et souvent mal-payé. Les étudiants doivent donc être très motivés, et chercher leur emploi avec conviction pour être choisis parmi le grand nombre de candidats qui souhaitent également gagner de l'argent durant les vacances.

# Dialogue 5
## Employability, working
*Yvonne talks about her part-time job.*

**Question :** Yvonne, vous travaillez le soir ou le weekend ?

**Yvonne :** Oui, les deux. Je travaille dans un bar le jeudi de 8h jusqu'à minuit, puis aussi le samedi pour huit heures en tout.

**Question :** Pourquoi est-ce que vous faîtes ce travail ?

**Yvonne :** Alors, il y a deux raisons : premièrement, je suis assistante dans une école à Glasgow, et mon appartement est très cher, donc je trouve que j'ai besoin de gagner un peu d'argent en plus. Et puis, ce qui est plus important, je peux sortir et rencontrer d'autres gens dans une bonne ambiance.

**Question :** Vous aimez votre petit boulot ?

**Yvonne :** Bien sûr : c'est bien payé. En plus je rencontre beaucoup de monde lorsque je suis dans le bar, et après le travail on sort pour aller à un club ensemble.

**Question :** Il n'y a pas de problèmes avec le travail ?

**Yvonne :** Eh oui, je dois admettre que le vendredi, quand je dois me lever tôt pour aller à l'école, je suis très fatiguée et il me faut beaucoup d'énergie avec mes classes. Et quelquefois il y a des gens qui ont trop bu dans le bar, et ça peut être gênant, mais c'est assez rare, quand même.

**Question :** Est-ce que vous avez travaillé chez vous en France, pendant que vous étiez en fac ?

**Yvonne :** Non, pas vraiment. J'habite encore chez mes parents, et pour cette raison je n'ai pas de loyer à payer, non plus pour manger. L'université est à deux kilomètres, donc le transport ne coûte pas cher.

**Question :** Alors vous vivez de votre argent de poche ?

**Yvonne :** Ah non, je travaille toujours pendant les grandes vacances, et je garde l'argent que je gagne : ça me

⇨

⇨

donne normalement tout l'argent qu'il me faut pour l'année universitaire.

**Question :** Qu'est-ce que vous faîtes comme travail ?

**Yvonne :** Je suis monitrice dans une colonie de vacances. Je fais cela pendant les mois de juillet et d'août. C'est génial, parce que tout est payé, ma chambre, les repas, et je ne dépense rien, seulement mon téléphone portable.

**Question :** Qu'est-ce que vous devez faire dans le travail ?

**Yvonne :** Alors, on travaille avec les enfants qui sont là pendant quatre semaines. Les enfants avec lesquels je travaille ont entre six et douze ans. On leur offre des activités sportives et culturelles, on reste avec eux quand ils mangent, on écoute leurs problèmes entre beaucoup d'autres devoirs : c'est fatigant, mais cela en vaut la peine, quand on voit les petits s'amuser tellement.

# Monologue 6
## Culture, working abroad

*You hear a podcast about French people who choose to live and work abroad.*

D'après les chiffres annoncés récemment, en dix ans, près de 600 milles Français sont partis à la recherche d'un emploi à l'étranger. Et encore ! L'ambassade de France en Chine annonçait récemment une hausse du pourcentage des jeunes expatriés (près de 100 chaque mois) venus s'installer définitivement, soit à la recherche d'un job d'été, d'un stage, ou d'un emploi. Travailler à l'étranger attire donc de plus en plus de jeunes diplômés affligés par le chômage en France ou attirés par des perspectives de carrières plus intéressantes que dans leur pays.

⇨

⇨

D'un autre côté aussi, il y a les personnes professionnelles qui espèrent le meilleur à l'étranger. Et bien évidemment, il y a des travailleurs, qui de plus en plus, trouvent intéressante l'idée d'aller voir plus loin, dans un nouvel environnement pour redynamiser leur carrière. Bien sûr, travailler à l'étranger est une décision qui mérite d'être prise avec beaucoup de soin. Seul le goût de l'aventure ne suffit plus.

Un travailleur qui regrette sa décision explique : « J'avais l'impression d'être exploité dans mon travail ici. En plus, je rêvais de partir à l'étranger. Je me disais qu'ailleurs, surtout dans un pays exotique, j'aurai plus de chances de me faire remarquer. J'ai donc réuni mes économies et j'ai fait le grand saut. Malheureusement, je n'ai rien trouvé d'intéressant. J'aieu une période difficile qui finalement m'a fait admettre que je n'avais pas été assez préparé. Je suis revenu au pays déçu. ».

# Dialogue 6
## Culture, working abroad
*Vincent talks about the differences between eating in France and in Scotland.*

**Question :** Vincent, vous êtes depuis un an ici en Écosse. Quelles sont pour vous les différences les plus marquantes entre la vie ici et la vie chez vous ?

**Vincent :** Je viens d'une ville dans le Midi, donc évidemment la différence la plus importante est le temps. Ici il pleut souvent, et il fait beaucoup plus froid, même en été. Mais à part cela je dirais que la plus grande différence est la façon de se nourrir.

**Question :** Vous pouvez expliquer un peu ?

**Vincent :** Ça commence avec le petit déjeuner. Chez nous, on prend un café ou un bol de chocolat avec du pain. On peut aussi trouver des céréales. Mais ici j'ai vu des gens commencer la journée avec un hamburger, ou un grand plat plein de saucissons, d'œufs au jambon. Puis je vois d'autres qui ne prennent rien sauf un coca.

**Question :** Vous l'avez essayé vous-même, le petit déjeuner anglais ?

**Vincent :** Ah non, je ne pourrais pas. J'ai déjà horreur des aliments trop gras, et le matin ça serait pire.

**Question :** Il y a d'autres différences ?

**Vincent :** Je dirais qu'il n'y a que des différences : à midi, pour déjeuner ici, la plupart de ceux que je rencontre ne s'arrêtent pas de travailler. Ils restent au bureau ⇨

⇨ avec un sandwich et une boisson, peut-être ils surfent un peu sur l'internet, mais c'est tout. Il y a d'autres qui sortent pour faire du jogging, et après ils mangent vite quelque chose en deux/trois minutes. Même les élèves des écoles dans les alentours, je les vois dans la rue à midi avec un sandwich ou des frites à la main, ils ne s'asseyent même pas.

**Question :** Et ce n'est pas votre habitude ?

**Vincent :** Bien sûr que non ! Quand j'étais au lycée, on avait une heure et demie pour déjeuner, et j'en profitais pour rentrer chez moi et manger dans le confort quelque chose qu'avait préparé ma mère.

**Question :** Et qu'est-ce que vous faîtes ici en Écosse ?

**Vincent :** Alors, on a une heure pour le déjeuner et je prends cette heure, je n'en sacrificie rien au travail, je me relâche. Je mange un plat cuisiné et un dessert, et après je prends un café. Je reste Français !

**Question :** Comment trouvez-vous les restaurants ici ?

**Vincent :** Là aussi je vois beaucoup de différences. Chez nous, la plupart des restaurants offrent un repas français, quoi. Il y a bien sûr des restaurants italiens et vietnamiens ou chinois, mais c'est à peu près tout. Ici, on a des difficultés à trouver un restaurant qui offre des plats écossais. Le plat principal écossais me semble être un curry.

**Question :** Qu'est-ce que vous en pensez ?

**Vincent :** Pour moi, je suis content : je peux expérimenter avec un tas de cuisines différentes : ici j'ai mangé pour la première fois dans un restaurant mexicain, et je mange regulièrement dans un restaurant végétarien, chose que je ne ferais jamais chez nous, même si ça existait.

# Monologue 7
## Culture, travel
*You hear this report about holiday planning.*

Partir en vacances est toujours enthousiasmant. Partir à l'étranger peut être source d'une légère anxiété. Préparer, prévoir et organiser son voyage évitera le stress de dernière minute et vous épargnera des soucis pendant cette belle période que sont les vacances. Quelques séances de natation, un peu de vélo, de marche à pieds, tout sera bon pour habituer vos muscles à l'exercice physique que vous pratiquerez pendant vos vacances, car si vous vous lancez sans entraînement, vous risquez votre santé. ⇨

Attention ! Les méfaits du soleil ne se limitent pas aux coups de soleil. Il accentue les rides, il favorise le vieillissement de la peau et pire, il peut être à l'origine de cancers de la peau. Protégez votre corps d'un T-shirt léger, d'un chapeau, vos yeux de lunettes de soleil de qualité. Ne faites pas trop confiance aux crèmes solaires. Certaines d'entre elles sont plus dangereuses que le soleil lui-même, à cause des produits cancérigènes qui les composent. D'autre part, elles vous donnent l'illusion que vous êtes bien protégé et vous poussent à passer trop de temps sous le soleil. Il est aussi important d'éviter les heures chaudes du milieu de journée.

Chaque année, des noyades transforment les vacances en tragédies. Il faut rester prudent, obéir aux consignes de sécurité sur les plages, respecter les couleurs des drapeaux rouges et verts sur la plage. Que ce soit à la mer ou en eau douce, entrez toujours progressivement dans l'eau. Mouillez-vous les bras, et si elle vous semble trop froide, sortez de l'eau. Evitez de nager seul.

# Dialogue 7
## Culture, travel

*Jacques talks about his experiences of holidays with his family and his friends.*

**Question :** Jacques, quand êtes-vous parti en vacances sans les parents pour la première fois ?

**Jacques :** Alors, ça dépend : je suis parti pratiquement chaque année dès l'âge de treize ans en colonie de vacances avec mes copains, normalement dans le Midi. Là, c'était une visite organisée, il y avait des moniteurs, ce n'était pas vraiment indépendant. La première fois que je suis parti avec mes copains indépendant, j'avais dix-sept ans.

**Question :** Où êtes-vous allés ?

⇨

**Jacques :** On est allés en Bretagne à vélo pour faire du camping, et on a passé une semaine près de Saint Malo. Nous étions quatre, tous en première au lycée. On a fait cinquante kilomètres par jour, mais nous restions toujours près de la mer, pour pouvoir nager chaque matin.

**Question :** Comment est-ce que ça vous a plu ?

**Jacques :** C'était super : on s'est levé tard le matin, il n'y avait pas de pression pour visiter les monuments, et nous avons mangé quand et comment nous voulions.

**Question :** Vous aimiez aller en vacances avec vos parents ?

**Jacques :** Ah oui, je m'entends bien avec ma famille, et on allait toujours à une petite maison dans le Midi, au bord de la mer. J'avais beaucoup de liberté, parce qu'on connaissait tout le monde dans le village, et j'avais des amis là-bas.

**Question :** Il n'y avait jamais de problèmes ?

**Jacques :** Si, il y avait des règlements pour les repas : je devais me lever à huit heures pour le petit déjeuner, et je devais toujour rentrer à une heure pour déjeuner, même si je voulais rester à la plage avec mes copains.

**Question :** Comment sont vos vacances aujourd'hui ?

**Jacques :** C'est bien varié : quelquefois je pars en train avec mes parents une semaine à la même maison, dans le Midi, mais je pars aussi avec ma petite amie un peu plus loin. On part en avion, pour aller en Grèce ou en Espagne.

**Question :** Êtes-vous actif en vacances ?

**Jacques :** Oui, bien que j'aime encore me lever tard. Mais je suis assez sportif, et j'aime pratiquer de nouveaux sports. L'année dernière j'ai appris la plongée sous-marine, et cette année je veux bien pratiquer de la planche à voile.

## What you should be able to do 👍

★ Answer questions, sometimes briefly, sometimes at length.
★ Ask your own questions.
★ Know how to ask for help (asking for the question to be repeated, saying you don't quite understand, etc.).
★ Be prepared to take your time and not rush (that includes knowing 'slowing' language).
★ Give opinions.

# Introduction

Talking is worth **25%** of your overall Higher result. You will have to carry out only one talking assessment, possibly in the spring term. This assessment will consist of an informal conversation about yourself to settle you into the assessment and a follow-up discussion with your teacher on two topics from different contexts. The topics for the conversation will be agreed by you and your teacher together, and the whole assessment will be marked by your teacher. It will be recorded and may be sent to SQA for assessment/moderation, or it may not. You will not know in advance whether it will be sent off, so just assume it will be.

The initial part of the assessment is intended to settle you, so there should not be challenging questions here. Things such as what you are studying, questions about your family or hobbies: nothing unexpected. You can also take this opportunity to ask your teacher a couple of questions on the same kind of topics about themselves. This initial part of the conversation could last up to two minutes, but if you are ready to move on from this to one of your topic areas, then take the initiative!

You and your teacher should discuss the topic areas you want to use in the conversation well in advance, so you have time to prepare them. You should choose areas you are comfortable with, but ones that allow you to display your knowledge of French and give you a chance to put in some good vocabulary and structures. Remember that the two topic areas you choose should come from two different contexts. They do not have to cover all the areas in a context, and of course if it is appropriate, you might include material from another context as well.

The rules for the assessment are quite clear: there will be an initial discussion, lasting about two minutes, which gives you a chance to start off the assessment well and confidently. You will be allowed to note a certain number of words (five headings of up to eight words each) to help you through your topics. Your conversation will be graded according to the criteria shown in Appendix 3, and that will let you see what is expected of you to reach each of the possible marks.

## Remember

☞ Recording yourself on a phone or tablet, then listening back with what you have said in front of you is a good way to improve your talking.

☞ If you have trouble remembering what you intend to say, try writing out key words to help you, or write it out with gaps to make a cloze passage that will guide you through what you want to say.

☞ In your discussion, you are allowed five groups of up to eight words to support you; choose these carefully and use them as a transition from one area to another.

☞ You can have them written out as cue cards, or in big letters so they don't make you stop to read them.

The whole conversation is marked out of 30 and is worth **25%** of your final mark. All parts of the conversation count towards the final grade, and if you perform better in one part than another, the final mark will reflect this.

In this chapter we will look at the two types of task in detail, and give you advice and support on preparing for the kind of task you are facing.

# The initial discussion

For this, you should have an idea of the kind of questions your teacher is going to ask you so you can prepare some good answers. It is intended to set you at ease, and the questions should not be too challenging, but it is the perfect opportunity for you to show off some good French, using some complex sentences and being able to answer at length, rather than just giving short answers. Remember, the whole conversation is assessed holistically, so make sure you shine right at the start. Prepare some answers for the simple questions you will be asked that show off how much you know about French.

You should be reasonably accurate in your use of French and use tenses and a variety of structures well. You are expected to expand beyond the kind of vocabulary and ideas you used at National 5. Your opinions are very important, and you should also include reasons for some of these opinions.

## Planning your talk

When you have two topics for your assessment, try to break them down into sections, and prepare each one separately: this will make it easier to remember, as well as giving you some structure. You are allowed five headings of eight words each as support, so these key words should help you into each section of your talk. This is handy as, if you get nervous and you get a bit mixed up in one part, you can recover in the next part with the help of your key words.

Once you've chosen your topic areas, focus on the actual language you will use. Below you will find a few dos and don'ts.

## Hints & tips ⭐

✓ **Do** look at the texts you have been working from for good ideas you can use. These texts will be at the level you should be working at.

✓ **Do** make sure you understand what you are saying, or it will be very difficult to remember it properly. Use complex language, yes, but only language you are comfortable with.

✓ **Do** think about your pronunciation: record yourself and listen to what you sound like. Could you sound more French?

✓ **Do** share your drafts with your teacher to get any suggestions or corrections made, and do this well in advance.

✓ **Do** use a variety of structures. Start collecting these in a notebook or in an area of your folder or computer.

⇨

✓ **Do** vary your tenses, and put in complex sentences, using a variety of different joining words or conjunctions like parce que, car or quand. If you can, use some of the conjunctions followed by the subjunctive (advice on this is in the structures and vocabulary chapter, Chapter 12, and you can also find examples in Chapter 9).

✓ **Do** give your opinion at every opportunity, and work at having different ways of saying what you think. Look at the 'Giving opinions and reasons' section in the chapter on structures and vocabulary (Chapter 12, page 96).

✓ **Do** also use adjectives and adverbs, some of these being attached to the nouns and verbs they are describing.

✓ **Don't** leave the preparation to the last minute. If you start your preparation early, you'll be able to ask your teacher for advice on any vocabulary or grammar you're unsure of. That means not just the week before, but a month before.

✓ **Don't** always stick to safe, simple language. It may be easier, but won't get the best grades. Try out some of the more impressive sentences you've come across. Note down useful vocabulary and phrases you've seen elsewhere under appropriate topic headings so you can reuse them in your talking tests.

✓ Just as at National 5, **don't** use lists of things, such as school subjects, places in town or favourite foods to try to make your talk longer: this will count against you.

## Choosing topics

The topic areas from which you will be working are the topic areas of the Higher Course, which are in Appendix 1. Remember that you will start on one topic area, then move on to another one. So have a plan ready for how and when to move on, and be ready for the situation where your teacher decides to move on! Discuss with your teacher how this will go, but remember you will not be expected to cover areas you have not yet dealt with in class as part of your Higher course.

How should you choose a topic? There are several points you should think about:

### Hints & tips ⭐

✓ Choose topic areas you are comfortable with, and know something about.

✓ Make sure your chosen areas allow you to get in a variety of tenses and structures, and allow you to put in opinions and feelings and explain the reasons for these opinions.

✓ Make sure it is not too simple, and only allows you to use the kind of language that would be appropriate for National 5: this is a particular danger with topics like family and school. Your daily routine, or what you are studying at school, are not able to give you enough chance to express yourself.

✓ You might want to choose topic areas you have been dealing with most recently, as they will be fresh in your mind.

✓ *You might want to start off on a small area of a topic you have dealt with, allowing you to broaden out into other aspects if you have time. In health, for instance, you could talk about the fact that so many girls smoke, and what can be done about it. This means you can go on to talk about diet, problems with drinking and drugs.*

# Remember

☞ Remember you need to know the question words, so you know what is being asked of you. Here are the main ones you will meet:

| | |
|---|---|
| Qui or Qui est-ce que | Who |
| Qu'est-ce que or Qu'est-ce qui | What |
| Quand or Quand est-ce que | When |
| Où or Où est-ce que | Where |
| Quel or Quelle | Which |
| Pourquoi or Pourquoi est-ce que | Why |
| Comment or Comment est-ce que | How |
| Combien | How much or how many |

☞ Remember that in English we use 'do' to make a question: 'do you have', 'do you know' and so on. In French, questions are normally made with est-ce que: est-ce que tu as, est-ce qu tu sais and so on. Let us look at making up questions. There are three main ways to do this:

1 Start with a question word if you need one. Add est-ce que. Then carry on with subject and verb as in a normal sentence.

2 Another way to ask a question is just to change the way you say a sentence, by making your voice rise at the end.

3 The third method is inversion, that is, changing the order of the subject and the object: Avez-vous ?

# The discussion of topics

If you can give full answers to the questions on the first topic, and also ask some questions of your own, then you should expect to answer something like 12 to 15 questions in the time allocated. Shorter answers will inevitably lead to more questions, and are less likely to let you show off all the things that will get you good grades.

You can decide when to move on to another topic, by letting your teacher know you are ready (in French, of course!). This makes it easy for the 'interlocutor', normally your teacher, to ask the first questions on the second topic area, and for you to have a chance to give answers based on the material you have been studying, and to refocus on the new area.

When preparing for the conversation, it is important that you allow yourself the opportunity to demonstrate your strengths, namely the control of structures and vocabulary, a variety of tenses, a structure to the answer, opinions and reasons, and so on. The best way to do this is to make your answers longer, which has the added advantage that you will have to answer fewer questions. If you have been able to think of longer answers, it also means that some of your answers can be quite short; this is useful when you cannot think of an answer, or you are going down a road the teacher is taking you, but you do not want to go!

One useful approach is the **one-two-three** approach: this means every answer should have three parts. If you are asked for instance, 'Qu'est-ce que vous allez faire dans votre boulot ?', then your answer could go:

> (1) Je vais travailler dans un supermarché qui s'appelle ...
>
> (2) Là, je travaillerai normalement à la caisse.
>
> (3) C'est un travail assez bien payé.

## Remember

☞ The initial two minutes are to allow you to get started successfully and settle your nerves.

☞ You can choose when to move on to the next area of the assessment (the discussion), which will start in one of the topic areas you have chosen. This is less predictable ...

This allows the next question to be one that asks you what you think of your job. Again, when giving your opinion, stick to the one-two-three approach:

> (1) Je trouve le travail dans le supermarché assez ennuyeux
>
> (2) parce que travailler à la caisse est très répétitif
>
> (3) mais mes copains travailleront là aussi, donc ça va tout de même.

This has given you the opportunity to give reasons and use conjunctions. You might also have prepared another answer; the answer to the question: *'Pendant combien de temps est-ce que vous avez travaillé là ?'* The one-two-three approach should make it easier to have longer answers, but it also makes it easier to remember your answers, as you can either count them off mentally or on your fingers as a memory aid. So, after having given one answer, you might think it a good chance to add another answer in here, and this is another way to help you control the conversation. Therefore, you could add this answer to the previous one, and it can still sound natural!

> (1) J'ai travaillé dans un supermarché pendant un mois.
>
> (2) J'ai commencé au mois de mai, après mes examens
>
> (3) parce que je voulais gagner de l'argent.

This answer also invites the question, 'What do you do with the money?', to which you would have prepared the answer in advance.

When discussing school or your future plans, an obvious question might be: *'Qu'est-ce que vous voulez faire après votre bac ?'* You have a choice here, as you could talk about your immediate plans, such as going on holiday with your friends, which allows you to develop this topic area, or you could talk about your plans to work, go to university or take a year out. If you stick to the latter, when you have said everything you can think of about university, and so on, you can then add to an answer a sentence such as, *'Mais dans le futur immédiat, je veux partir en vacances avec mes copines cet été'*. This will lead the conversation on to this area, which you can have prepared.

Let us look at another one-two-three answer to the question about your future plans:

> (1) Je ne suis pas certain de ce que je ferai.
>
> (2) Ou je pourrais aller directement à l'université, si je réussis à mes examens.
>
> (3) Ou je pourrai trouver un travail pour un an, les deux possibilités ont des avantages et des désavantages.

Again, this leads the conversation where you want. You can have prepared answers about the advantages and disadvantages, which allows you to get in good structures, reasons and opinions. And remember, when you think you have exhausted this topic, you can lead on to the next area: the immediate future.

When discussing holidays, or families, a reasonable question might be: '*Comment est-ce que vous vous entendez avec vos parents ?*' Even if you are not asked this question, you will always be able to squeeze in the answer by saying at some point, '*Mais quand même, j'aime les voyages avec mes parents, car on s'entend bien,*' and then going on to give your prepared answer. Here is a possible one-two-three answer to the question:

> (1) Généralement, on s'entend très bien, je crois
>
> (2) bien que ce soit de temps en temps un peu difficile (*or:* bien sûr c'est de temps en temps un peu difficile,)
>
> (3) surtout quand je rentre trop tard le soir, mes parents s'inquiètent.

This has allowed you to put in a subjunctive, if you want, and put together a structured answer. Another possible question was about your friends: it may go something like this: '*Est-ce que vous avez beaucoup d'amis ?*' The one-two-three answer could be:

> (1) Oui, nous sommes un grand groupe de copains, tous à l'école,
>
> (2) et nous faisons beaucoup de choses ensemble
>
> (3) mais évidemment j'ai deux copines qui me sont plus proches.

This answer lets you invite the next question, about the two special friends, which you can either wait for, or just insert the answer here to give you a much longer answer.

What is really important about the conversation is that it flows, and is a real conversation: you have to really answer the questions that are put to you, and to ask some of your own. For this to happen, you must be very confident you understand the question put to you, and know how to ask questions. When you have asked a question, respond to your teacher's answer, to make it more of a real conversation. That might simply be '*Ah, je vois !*' or '*Oui, je suis d'accord avec vous*'. If you do not understand the question, don't try to bluff or guess, and do not under any circumstances blurt out an answer you have learned and hope for the best! It is much better to ask for help in French, and if you ask properly, you need not bring your grade down at all; in fact, you might be able to help it get better, as this is part of what is called 'sustaining the conversation'.

## Hints & tips

Here are some ways of asking for help, starting off easy and getting more complicated, but better.

✓ Pardon ?
✓ Voulez-vous répéter, s'il vous plaît ?
✓ Je n'ai pas compris, exactement.
✓ Là, je n'ai pas compris : pourriez-vous répéter la question ?
✓ Excusez-moi, pourriez-vous reposer la question ? Je ne suis pas certain de ce que vous voulez savoir.

# Directed writing

## What you should be able to do 👍

★ Read the bullet points carefully.
★ Check when you have finished that you have answered each bullet point.
★ Make sure your tenses and verb endings are correct by using your dictionary.
★ Use a variety of structures.
★ Be ready to search through your memory for answers that fit the questions, rather than using the dictionary to look up new words.

# Introduction

There are two pieces of writing in Higher French. You will carry out a writing assignment in class and you will have to write a description of a trip you made to a French-speaking country. This is called Directed writing. The Directed writing tasks are given to you at the same time as the Reading and translation paper: you have up to 60 minutes to plan, write and proofread your piece. This is very achievable, as much of what you will have to write is predictable, and you can plan for this in advance.

The task will be based on a scenario given in English. The first decision you will have to make is which of two scenarios to choose to write about, as you will be faced with two from two different contexts. You will be required to provide specified information in a piece of writing of 150 to 180 words. You will be able to use a dictionary while doing the exam. The scenario always involves you describing a trip to, or an experience in, a French-speaking country, which took place some time in the past. This is to make sure you write in the past, and demonstrate your mastery of all the past tenses! Remember that when using the perfect tense, as well as adjectives, sometimes it will matter whether you are male or female, so make sure your endings are consistent.

The scenario is always given with six bullet points that you have to cover.

You can use textbooks and work you have already produced to guide you in your preparation, and you can work from guidelines provided by your teacher. This means you can really plan out a lot of what you want to write before the day of the exam.

Your writing will be graded according to how well it demonstrates a sense of structure, control of grammar, and how it addresses the bullet points. The way of judging how well you have done is given in the marking schemes for directed writing. These are in Appendix 4, and will let you see what is expected of you. You will achieve a grade based on the quality of your writing, and then you will lose marks for each bullet point, or part of a bullet point, you miss out. This means it is important you do not miss out any bullet points, and address each one in your writing. Tick them off on your exam paper as you go, to make sure you have covered every one, and indeed each part of them.

## Hints & tips ⭐

✓ This part of the exam you can really prepare for: you should probably know 80% of what you will write before you go into the exam.

✓ It is probably a good idea to start off with this before you tackle the Reading.

✓ If you do this, and find one bullet point is taking too long, leave it, go to the Reading, and come back to it later.

✓ Remember that using 'additional relevant information' is a positive thing, so be ready to include things that are not directly asked for, but you know are good French and can be seen as relevant.

# Sample paper
## An example

Let us look at an example of a directed writing paper. After this, we will look at the kind of general basic answers you should be prepared to write, which should help you write an essay based on this question. When you have done that, take it to your teacher and ask them (very nicely, of course!) to mark it.

## Question ❓

### Scenario 1: Employability

You have recently returned from France, where you have had a summer job.

On your return, you have been asked to write an account of your experiences to try to encourage other students to do the same thing.

**You must include** the following information and **you should try to add** other relevant details:

- What your job was **and** what you thought of it
- How you travelled to France
- What you had to do in your job
- What you liked/disliked about the people you worked with
- What you did in your spare time
- If you would recommend such an experience to others

## Question ❓

### Scenario 2: Culture

Last year you went with your school/college to a town in France for a few days.

While you were there you went shopping.

On your return you were asked to write a report, **in French**, of your visit.

**You must include** the following information and **you should try to add** other relevant details:

- Where you went **and** what you thought of the accommodation
- What the weather was like
- What you did while you were there
- How you got on with people you met
- What you liked/disliked most about the experience
- Whether you plan to return there in the future

Your first decision is which scenario to choose, and you should make this decision quickly. When you have done so, put a line through the other one, so you do not make a mistake and answer bits from both! The reason for your choice should be: which one do I have most points with answers already prepared?

You will see that there are six bullet points you have to cover, as well as bearing in mind the instructions in the box. This means you cannot simply prepare a piece of writing, learn it, and then write it out again in the exam.

There are four possible contexts, but only two will be on offer in the exam. Some of the bullet points are predictable, but others will be unique to that exam, so you will have to be ready to be flexible. You have to write 150 to 180 words in total, so a good rule of thumb is that each bullet point should have 25 to 30 words, with one or two being a bit longer. If your writing is unbalanced, you might lose points. This guideline also makes it easier to keep track of how much you are writing, rather than always recounting words and wasting time. It is really important to notice that the first bullet point has two parts, both parts of which you must answer, or you will lose marks.

# Scenario 1

Let us look at the first scenario:

- *What your job was and what you thought of it*

For this, you know it was a summer job, so you can start off with a general introduction, then choose a job you have perhaps already done at home, as you will have the vocabulary for this. For part two, go for a positive and a negative viewpoint, to vary your structures and to allow you to use more pre-learned material:

Cette année, au mois de juin, je suis partie pour aller à Lille, dans le nord-est de la France. Là, j'ai travaillé dans un café comme serveuse. Les autres serveuses étaient très sympathiques, mais le patron était un peu sévère. Quand même je me suis bien amusée.

Opinions are always worth fitting in, as you can have the sentences ready, with just a word or two to alter. Note that this has been answered as a girl, so all the endings agree with that.

- *How you travelled to France*

This is something you should always have ready, as even if you are not asked for it, it fits as 'other relevant information'. You should always be ready to take an opportunity to give your opinion about the journey, whether positive, negative, or both!

J'ai pris le train pour aller en France, parce que j'ai rendu visite à ma tante qui habite à Paris. Le voyage était long, mais je me suis bien amusée, car j'ai parlé français avec mes voisins dans le train.

- *What you had to do in your job*

You can use simple points, but make them more complex by adding sub-clauses with opinions, which again you can have ready and just fit in. Do not use lists; just a couple of points with opinions:

J'ai dû servir les clients dans le café et sur la terrasse, ce qui était très bien, parce que je parlais beaucoup de français. De temps en temps je faisais la vaisselle dans la cuisine, mais je n'aimais pas ça, car il y faisait très chaud.

- *What you liked/disliked about the people you worked with*

You have already mentioned likes and dislikes, but go on to do something similar here:

Les autres serveuses étaient très sympathiques, mais le patron était un peu sévère. J'ai beaucoup appris dans son café, parce qu'il m'a montré comment servir les clients. Quand même je me suis bien amusée.

- *What you did in your spare time*

This is another area you should always have ready, as it comes up very often. Just remember that it should fit in with the time of year you were there, so have winter and summer possibilities ready. And, of course, have your opinions and thoughts included!

Le weekend je suis sortie souvent avec mes copines du café, ce que j'aimais beaucoup. Une fois nous sommes allées au cinéma pour voir un film français. J'ai trouvé ça difficile à comprendre ! J'ai également passé des heures dans les grands magasins !

- *If you would recommend such an experience to others*

This is almost certainly going to come up, so be ready for this. Think future and conditional tenses, and have a set of phrases ready to use:

J'ai tellement apprécié ma visite que je recommanderais un tel emploi aux élèves écossais. C'était une visite très réussie. Je voudrais y retourner l'année prochaine, parce que, comme ça, je parlerai plus de français et je pourrai améliorer mon accent.

# Scenario 2

Now have a look at the second scenario, and see how you can adapt the answer above to fit that.

- *Where you stayed and what you thought of the accommodation*

You can use the same first sentence, and vary the answer to fit the bullet point:

L'année dernière, au mois de décembre, je suis partie pour aller à Lille, dans le nord-est de la France. Là, je suis restée dans un hôtel avec les autres de ma classe. L'hôtel était très agréable, mais le patron était un peu sévère. Quand même je me suis bien amusée.

- *What the weather was like*

This is another area worth preparing, as it would certainly fit under 'other relevant details', as long as you made sure the weather was right for the time given. Again, your opinions matter and offer you the chance to put in sub-clauses.

Parce que c'était au mois de décembre, il ne faisait pas un temps splendide ! Il a beaucoup plu, et il faisait froid. Mais ce n'était pas important, parce que le temps était comme chez nous.

**or**

On était là au mois de juin, et il faisait un temps splendide ! Le soleil brillait chaque jour, il faisait chaud, et tout le monde était bien content, parce qu'il faisait bien meilleur qu'en Écosse !

- *What you did while you were there*

Nous avons visité un café et tous les petits magasins, ce qui était très bien, parce que je parlais beaucoup de français. Nous avons acheté beaucoup de cadeaux pour nos familles, car il y avait des choses très différentes de chez nous.

- *How you got on with the people you met*

It is always worth having an answer ready for this, as the question comes up so often. It is worth having two answers ready, one for people you got on well with (and why) and one for people you did not get on so well with.

Nous avons rencontré des jeunes Français dans un café et nous avons parlé franglais avec eux, ce qui était très amusant. Mais je n'ai pas du tout aimé les gens dans notre hôtel, parce qu'ils n'étaient pas très gentils.

- *What you liked/disliked most about the experience*

Le patron de l'hôtel était assez sévère, mais j'ai beaucoup aimé notre séjour, parce que l'hôtel était très propre. Je n'aimais pas beaucoup le temps, parce qu'il faisait assez froid, mais j'adorais parler avec tous les jeunes Français que j'ai rencontrés.

- *Whether you plan to return there in the future*

This last bullet point always asks either about the future or whether you would recommend such a visit to others. It is worth having both future and conditional tenses ready, as almost certainly both will fit. Giving reasons such as 'I learned lots of French', or 'I had a really great time' will also always fit in. Saying you plan to return next year is also almost always going to work.

L'année prochaine je vais retourner en France avec des amis, parce qu'on s'est si bien amusés. Nous allons rencontrer nos amis français. Personnellement, je recommanderais une telle visite à tout le monde, car on apprend beaucoup de français dans un temps très court.

# Preparing for writing

What will you find easiest to prepare? Here is a list of things that are liable to come up: and remember, if they do not come up, you can still use your prepared material as 'other relevant details'.

- ☞ **How you got there**
  (you can prepare this in advance, but be ready to change methods of transport and times or dates)
- ☞ **What you thought of the people you were with**
  (have a positive and a negative sentence ready for this)
- ☞ **What the journey was like**
- ☞ **Where you stayed and what you thought of it**
  (this could be the house, the hostel, the town or the area)
- ☞ **What you did when you were there**
  (this is an area where you will have to have different ideas ready, as you may be on a work experience, school exchange, sports trip, school visit, family visit, and so on)
- ☞ **What you thought of what you were doing**
  (have a positive and a negative opinion ready)                    ⇨

⇨
☞ *What you did in the evenings (more predictable!)*
☞ *What you thought of the place or people you stayed or worked with*
☞ *Whether you will do such a visit again, and why (this makes you put in a future or conditional tense)*
☞ *How you will keep in touch with people you met*

Let's look at some of these, one at a time.

# How you got there

Only one of the scenarios exemplified above specifies this, but it counts as 'other relevant details', so it is worth having a sentence ready.

If we assume you went to France, you can choose your method of transport, unless the question actually specifies the method. You should also be able to put in when you went, as this is relevant. However, you might also have to change these details. This is liable to be the start to your writing, so start off well to impress the examiner:

> L'année dernière, au mois de juin, je suis parti pour aller à Lille, dans le nord-est de la France. Nous sommes allés en train.

This is quite straightforward, and would lead into most scenarios. We have also varied the subject and the structures, so that every sentence does not start off with *je*. Note, this is for a boy.

This part should be short, and would only go on if you were asked to describe the journey, as it could otherwise be seen as using irrelevant material. You must make sure your answers are relevant to the questions asked.

# Where you stayed

This might be a family home, or hostel or other accommodation. If staying with a family, this can be very straightforward; just a simple description of the house and your room with of course, as usual, an opinion:

> Ma famille habitait une petite maison qui avait trois chambres, à deux kilomètres de l'école. Moi, j'avais ma propre chambre, et j'en étais content, car chez moi je dois partager une chambre avec mon frère.

If you are in student accommodation, the answer can be very similar:

> Je logeais dans un bâtiment à deux kilomètres de l'université. Moi, j'avais une petite chambre pour moi, et j'en étais content, car chez moi je dois partager une chambre avec mon frère.

# What you did when you were there

This will depend very much on the scenario set at the top of the task, but there will still be common structures you can use throughout the different scenarios. There are two different areas here as well: the first is what you did during the day; the second is what you did in your leisure time.

Firstly let us look at what you could write about the daytime. This will depend very much on whether you are describing a visit to a school, family, and so on, or whether you are working. If you are visiting someone, then you will be able to use the following kind of language:

> Tous les jours on a fait des visites : on est allés par exemple au centre-ville de Lille pour voir les musées, et l'on a fait une visite en bus à une brasserie, où l'on a pu essayer de la bière française : c'était amusant de voir nos profs avec un verre à la main, et j'ai pris une photo pour faire chanter [*blackmail!*] Mme Vernier !

If you are visiting a family, use this as an opportunity to use third-person verbs, as well as *nous* and *on*, as this gets away from always using *je*. Note that this answer is for a boy; for a girl, probably use *ma corres* or ma copine (mon copain) and *emmenée*:

> Les parents de mon corres m'ont emmené en Belgique, où l'on a pris un bateau-mouche à Bruges : c'était extra, car on a vu tous les canaux.

If you are attending a school, then you can describe the school, the teachers and what you thought of some of the lessons:

> Le lycée était très grand : il y avait 1800 élèves en tout dans un bâtiment immense, et tellement de professeurs que je ne reconnaissais personne. J'ai participé à des cours d'anglais (marrant) et de maths (épatant). On n'a pas pu faire du sport, ce qui était dommage.

If you are working, or taking part in work experience, then you can describe your job and what you thought of it. Note that this answer is for a girl:

> J'ai travaillé dans un hôtel comme serveuse, ce qui était assez difficile, car tout le monde parlait en français, bien sûr. Le travail était dur, mais j'ai reçu beaucoup de pourboires, donc j'étais très contente finalement.

## What you did in the evenings

You are also likely to be asked to write what you did during your free time, in the evenings or at the weekends. The following answers are all for a male writer. This might be mixed up with what you did generally, but you can probably use this section whatever the topic. Here is one suggestion, but you should prepare your own and have it ready to use:

Je suis allé au cinéma une fois avec un groupe de copains : pour moi, c'était la première fois que j'ai vu un film en français sans sous-titres, et je n' ai pas compris grand-chose.

## What you thought of the place or people you stayed or worked with

You are very likely to be asked about your impressions of the other people there, or how you got on with them, or else what you thought of where you stayed. This is pretty predictable, with just a few changes necessary to meet the context. For instance, for your fellow students:

Je me suis très bien entendu avec les autres étudiants. Ils étaient tous sympa, et nous restons en contact par mail et par sms. Surtout j'ai aimé Vincent, qui a passé beaucoup de temps avec moi, et qui m'a aidé à parler français.

Or your host family:

Je me suis très bien entendu avec ma famille. Ils étaient tous sympa, et nous restons en contact par mail et par lettre. Surtout j'ai aimé la mère de mon corres, qui a passé beaucoup de temps avec moi, et qui m'a aidé à parler français.

## Whether you will do such a visit again, and why/How you will keep in touch with people you met

Usually you will be asked as a final bullet point to use the future and/or conditional tenses, by saying how you will keep in touch, whether you would do the visit again or how you will be helped in the future by your experience. This could be done by giving your plans for next year; saying when you will complete the exchange, or go back to the same place; describing how you will keep in touch; or by saying how much better your French is and what a confident mature person you have become! First of all, plans for the future:

En septembre mon corres (copain) reviendra chez nous avec sa classe : ils vont passer dix jours dans notre école, ce qui sera fantastique ! Pour l'instant, on va s'écrire des mails chaque semaine, et bien sûr j'enverrai des SMS (messages texte) s'il reste du crédit dans mon portable ! L'année prochaine, je voudrais bien retourner là-bas tout seul pour passer l'été à travailler et à apprendre plus de français.

And now you can boast about how wonderful your French has become! Into this you can even manage to get a subjunctive – *bien que j'aie*:

J'ai parlé beaucoup, et bien que j'aie fait pas mal d'erreurs, j'ai aussi fait de sérieux progrès. Cela m'aidera l'année prochaine, car je compte aller à l'université pour faire des études de français.

# Conclusion

So, hopefully you can see that the directed writing is not just a leap in the dark: most of the bullet points you can be well prepared for, as long as you are able to be flexible. Now try to write your own answer for one of the scenarios in the sample paper on page 76 and show your work to your teacher.

What you should do next is to look at the directed writing in other past or practice papers, which you can either buy, download from the SQA website, or ask your teacher to show you. Look at the bullet points in each of them, and see how much of each of these papers you can prepare in advance. You should also look at the bullet points that present unexpected material, and plan how you would answer them.

# Assignment-writing

## What you should be able to do 👍

- ★ Know what an essay structure looks like.
- ★ Know how to use a variety of grammar structures, vocabulary and sub-clauses.
- ★ Write an introduction.
- ★ Use arguments.
- ★ Come to a suitable conclusion.

# Introduction

As part of your Higher, remember you will have to produce two pieces of writing, which altogether makes up **25%** of your overall mark. The assignment is one of these two pieces; it is marked out of 20, and is worth **12.5%** of your final mark. It is a piece of writing that you will write in class under supervision. There is no time limit set for how long you take to write it, but you are expected to write between 200 and 250 words. However, there is no penalty if you go below or above this limit. Your teacher will discuss with you what topics you might like to write about (from any of the four contexts: Society, Learning, Employability or Culture) and then give you, on the day you start to produce the assignment, a question to discuss. If you have thought about more than one topic, then there will be a choice of questions for you to work from. There will be an initial question (in English) to start you off, and below this there will be a couple of supplementary questions to guide you through the topic. However, you have a great deal of freedom as to what you actually write, as long as in part of your answer you do actually address the questions set.

As support in your writing, you are allowed the following items:
- grammar reference notes (including verb tables)
- dictionary
- word lists on the topic you will be writing about
- the question your teacher has set you (the writing stimulus).

You do not have to finish the assignment that day; you can hand it back to your teacher at the end of the lesson and return to it later, which means you can go away and think some more about it. You will not see the exact questions until the day you have to start writing, but you will know what the topics are, and you should make a point of collecting relevant phrases and sentences on the topics you cover to give you a bank of material to work from when preparing these tasks.

Once you have completed your writing, you will hand it to your teacher: this is called a first draft. Your teacher will look at it and suggest how you might improve it: this is likely to include both comments and signs or symbols from a writing code. You can then go away and think about how to do so. When you are ready to write the final piece of work, you will be given your first draft along with the comments your teacher has made to work from. You will also have the same support as the first time, along with a writing code if you have been using one. There is an example of a writing code at the end of this chapter (see p.94).

Once you complete the second draft, your teacher will collect it, along with the question set and a note of which context it is from, before submitting it to SQA for marking. You will be asked to sign it to say it is all your own work.

Your writing should be a piece of 'discursive' writing: that means it should include an argument. It could be a discussion, presenting and comparing two points of view, then coming to a conclusion, or it could be a 'persuasive' essay, in which you take a point of view and defend it, showing how arguments against it are wrong.

Your writing will be marked according to its content, the accuracy of your language and the quality and variety of language and structure you use. The way of judging how well you have done is given in the criteria for Assignment-writing, Appendix 4. Looking at these will enable you to see what is expected of you if you are aiming for a specific mark. Looking more closely at these three criteria, we can see that:

- **Content** involves how well you communicate your ideas and opinions, the range of ideas and opinions you give, having a clear focus for your writing, using a structure that gives more than one point of view and finally draws conclusions.
- **Accuracy** is concerned with your correct use of grammar (particularly verbs) and spelling (think about your accents).
- The **language resource** is about how well you use your French, with a variety of structures and tenses: the vocabulary should not be too simple, you should use a number of different tenses, and a number of complex sentences, that is, sentences with a conjunction and a sub-clause, as well as adverbs attached to verbs and adjectives attached to nouns.

A good idea is to start off by writing a brief plan in French. This should have an introduction, the arguments you are going to use, any counterarguments, and, most importantly, a conclusion. It is also important to write in paragraphs, so one paragraph for the introduction, another three or four paragraphs for the main body and a short paragraph for the conclusion.

## Choosing a topic

From the context of learning, let us look at how to prepare to discuss the importance of languages for the future, which fits with the fact you have chosen to study Higher French, and should allow you to introduce material you will know well. This could be a persuasive essay, in which you try to persuade people of something you believe in. The question might look like:

## Question ❓

**How important will languages be for young people in Scotland in the future?**

How important are they to you?

Do you see yourself using your languages for work or leisure?

You should write an introduction and a conclusion, which would mean you have good structure to your writing. The introduction could be just a rephrasing of the question in English.

So, you might start off with something like this:

> Je voudrais examiner l'importance de connaître au moins une langue étrangère pour les jeunes Écossais dans l'avenir. Est-ce que tout le monde devrait parler une autre langue que la sienne ? Si oui, pourquoi ?

You might then carry on in response to the first sub-question:

> À mon avis, les langues étrangères sont très importantes pour nous en Écosse. J'apprends le français, bien sûr, parce que c'est nécessaire pour ce que je veux faire. Je fais aussi de l'espagnol, parce que c'est une langue que l'on parle partout en Amérique.

This is about 40 words and, although it is very simple and straightforward, it does answer the question and also allows you to include sub-clauses and adjectives, which show you can use structures.

You can now answer the second sub-question, about your own future use of languages.

> J'ai décidé que j'irai en fac l'année prochaine pour faire des études. Je voudrais étudier la biologie, parce que je m'y intéresse beaucoup, mais je pense que mon français me sera utile, parce que je pourrai faire un stage Erasmus+.

This answer is not complex, but it includes a variety of tenses and structures. You have answered all the questions and written 120 words. So now you have the opportunity to put in counterarguments, and then dismiss them. That should give you another 80 or more words and complete the structure, which gets you good marks.

> J'ai des amis qui pensent que ce n'est pas important d'apprendre une autre langue. Ils disent que tout le monde parle anglais, et que l'anglais est la langue de commerce internationale. Les étrangers doivent parler anglais lorsqu'ils sont en Écosse, mes amis disent qu'ils ne travailleront jamais à l'étranger, et que, comme touristes, ils s'attendent à ce que les gens qui travaillent dans le secteur de tourisme parlent anglais.
>
> Mais j'ai déjà visité la France, et je sais que ce n'est pas vrai. En plus, si l'on parle leur langue, les gens sont beaucoup plus accueillants.

This gives you an argument and a counterargument, as well as allowing you to use complex sentences, a variety of tenses, some conjunctions with sub-clauses and some adjectives attached to nouns: it also allows you to write in the third person, thus avoiding using *je* all the time. All of these are techniques that attract the best marks.

Finally, have a sentence ready to finish off with as a conclusion:

> Bref, je suis content(e) d'être prêt(e) pour l'avenir. Je suis content(e) de savoir que je vais utiliser mes langues dans l'avenir, et qu'elles seront utiles pour moi.

## Planning your writing

So, how can you best prepare for this writing assignment? Discuss with your teacher what areas or topics you would like to write about. Learn some really good material, use it appropriately and be straightforward when answering the specific questions, as this is likely to allow you to cover some areas you have prepared to write for, which should be in good French. Remember, you should answer the specific questions, but you are allowed to put in your own material as well, as long as it is relevant.

Have a bank of material on each of the main topic areas you have agreed. This could well include the material you prepared for your talking assessment, so look at Chapter 9 (Talking) for some ideas. Look also at the textbook or texts you are working from for good ideas you can use and find a good place to store these (this might be part of your folder, a special exercise book or on your computer). The listening transcripts from past Higher papers, as well as in this book, are also a good source of material, as they are at the right level and are examples of people giving opinions and reasons for these opinions.

## Hints & tips ⭐

- ✓ Choose topic areas you are comfortable with and know something about.
- ✓ Make sure your chosen areas allow you to include a variety of tenses and structures, as well as opinions and feelings, and explain the reasons for these opinions.
- ✓ Make sure your writing is not too simple and only allows you to use the kind of language appropriate for National 5: this is a particular danger with topics such as family and school, your daily routine or what you are studying at school – they are not able to give you enough chance to express yourself.
- ✓ You might want to choose topic areas you have been dealing with most recently, as they will be fresh in your mind.
- ✓ You might want to focus on a small area of a topic you have dealt with, allowing you to answer questions on this, but expand on it in the writing assignment. In health, for instance, you could talk about the fact that so many young people smoke, and what can be done about it. This means you can go on to write about diet, problems with drinking and drugs.

# Examples of planning

Let us look at some possible topics. The next section will guide you through the process involved in preparing for and carrying out the assessment for three specific topics. You can follow the same pattern for a writing assignment of your own choice.

## 1 Le tabagisme et les jeunes

### Question ❓

**Is smoking a real issue for young people today?**

Do you know people who smoke?

What are the dangers for young people?

This topic comes from the Society context and covers an aspect of young people's problems. Using this as a topic will allow you to write in both the first and the third person, give opinions and justify these and use good phrases from the texts you are working from. It should also allow you to give conflicting points of view. That means it will be a discursive essay, with a conclusion at the end.

Your first task should be a kind of brainstorming: look at your source texts and select a variety of really good phrases or ideas. Look at these in turn and try to identify a pattern or storyline to follow and give your presentation some structure. Then, break your task into areas. You could start with a section in which you talk about the importance of health, then have a section in which you talk about the dangers that smoking poses (and include a reference to what you think yourself), move on to where there are problems with this and finish off with what people (and you) should be doing to improve things. If you have a textbook, you could use this for source material, or you could look on the internet for supporting material.

The first section might read something like this:

> Est-ce que le tabagisme est un grand problème pour moi et pour mes amis ? De nos jours, l'on parle beaucoup de l'importance de la santé pour les jeunes : on pense à la nourriture dans les cantines scolaires, on essaie d'interdire aux gens de fumer dans les lieux publics, il y a beaucoup de publicité à la télévision et au cinéma pour persuader les gens d'arrêter de fumer.

This allows you to introduce the topic and has used the main question in English as the start. It also is general, and so avoids using *je* for just now. The second section can then let you move from the general to the particular, as in this example:

> Il est important de penser aux dangers pour les jeunes qui pensent à fumer, et l'une des choses les plus importantes est de les persuader de ne pas commencer. Lorsqu'on commence, il est souvent difficile d'arrêter. De plus, ça coûte cher, car les cigarettes prennent tout son argent, et parce qu'on pue le vieux tabac, personne ne veut s'asseoir à côté de vous.

This has allowed you to give opinions and justify them. You also have put in a sub-clause and some adjectives and adverbs.

The next section allows you to give some structure by moving to problems, to the other side of the discussion and also to personalise the discussion:

> Je le trouve quelquefois assez difficile d'éviter le tabac : souvent j'ai des amis qui veulent expérimenter, et je ne veux pas les perdre. Des fois quand je sors avec mes copains, il y en a un ou deux qui fument et boivent trop de bière, et je n'ai plus envie de sortir. Je préfère dans ce cas rester à la maison.

It is important to add in the little words and phrases that make your French flow better: words such as *quand même*, *quelquefois* and *assez*.

For the final section, you need to come to a conclusion, as well as giving an answer to the problems in the third paragraph. In this section, it is a chance to show off all the ways you know of expressing opinions and making demands:

Personnellement, je trouve qu'il vaut mieux montrer aux élèves à l'école les poumons des personnes qui fument, pour voir exactement les effets sur son corps. Je sais que beaucoup de jeunes ferment les yeux, mais il faut tout de même persister, car la santé est tellement importante pour notre avenir : il serait trop facile de faire ce qu'ont fait nos parents. Nous devons donc changer la manière dont nous menons nos vies, si nous voulons devenir un pays sain.

## 2 Boulot et bac

**Question**

**Is it important for young people to have part-time or summer jobs?**

Can it interfere with schoolwork?

Does it give experience of the world of work?

This topic comes from the Learning and Employability areas and allows you to write about both school and a summer job. It will link into your future, allowing you to use future tenses. It will be, like the previous task, a discursive essay, giving two sides of the argument before coming to a conclusion. Think about how you are going to structure your answer. Perhaps you might start off saying how you find studying and what your goals are. Then you could move on to talking about your job, saying where you are going to work. The next section could be about the clashes that sometimes occur for people doing part-time jobs, and you might finish off with the hope that it will all work out right in the end! Let's look at the first section, and remember not to go for lists in this area:

Les petits boulots, est-ce qu'ils sont une bonne idée pour moi et pour mes copains ? À présent je prépare mes Highers, l'équivalent du bac, afin de pouvoir aller plus tard à l'université, si je réussis. J'étudie cinq Highers, et il me faut faire deux heures de devoirs chaque soir, et même le weekend aussi ! Donc je n'ai pas de petit boulot, car je trouve que cela m'empêcherait de réussir à mes examens. Il m'est important d'avoir de bonnes notes pour aller à l'université de Glasgow.

This introduction, while not directly answering the question, is still relevant. It has given you the chance to put in some opinions, a hope and reasons. In the next section you can try to move away from just *je* and use the third person to give a better variety of structures. It also gives you the chance to vary your tenses:

> La plupart des élèves dans ma classe ont quand même un petit boulot. Ils travaillent pour gagner de l'argent, car comme ça on peut se payer des vêtements ou sortir le weekend. Le boulot leur offre de l'indépendance : ils ne dépendent plus de leurs parents pour leur argent de poche. Moi, j'ai travaillé dans un supermarché deux soirs par semaine, pendant un mois, mais c'était trop pour moi.

This is more of an answer to the questions set and gives one side of your argument. You can then go on to answer the first sub-question and have the other side of your discussion:

> Mes copains de classe et du travail ont quelquefois d'assez grands problèmes à combiner les devoirs et le boulot : souvent il arrive que l'on doit faire des heures supplémentaires le même jour que l'on a un devoir pour le prof d'anglais. Si l'on refuse les heures supplémentaires, on risque de perdre son emploi, mais évidemment si l'on ne prépare pas ses devoirs, on risque la colère du prof, et de ne pas réussir à ses examens.

Remember to keep putting in the little extra words, such as *assez* and *évidemment*, which make your language flow better. Moving on to the last section, this is a chance to change tenses and introduce conditional and future, as well as a subjunctive if you feel comfortable with this. This works as your conclusion as well:

> Naturellement je veux moi aussi gagner mon propre argent, donc je travaillerai cet été pendant six semaines dans un magasin, pour éviter des conflits entre les études et le travail. Mon espoir est que je continuerai à réussir, et je voudrais bien continuer de gagner de l'argent, mais je n'aimerais pas que mes notes souffrent à cause de mon boulot. Je ferai donc bien attention dans l'avenir, parce que pour moi le plus important sera de pouvoir aller en fac l'année prochaine.

## 3 Les voyages

### Question ?

**Are holidays important to you?**

Who do you like to go on holiday with?

What are your plans for this year?

This topic comes from the context Culture and allows you to bring in a variety of tenses and structures, mentioning past visits and your future plans. This will be a persuasive essay, but with a couple of negative points that you can brush aside! You might start with a general statement about how you love travelling, and why, then move on to a mention of a journey you particularly liked or disliked, finishing up with your plans for next summer, mentioning who you are travelling with. The first section, the introduction, could look like this:

Est-ce que j'aime aller en vacances ? Bien sûr ! J'habite dans une petite ville en Écosse, et je l'aime bien, mais quand même j'adore faire des voyages, surtout de longs voyages à l'étranger. J'aime voyager pour un tas de raisons, d'abord parce que j'aime les voyages eux-mêmes, être dans un train ou un avion. J'aime aussi rencontrer des gens que je ne connais pas, me faire de nouveaux amis. Finalement j'aime pouvoir parler une autre langue.

That section allows you to put together a list of three reasons, but to introduce them with different words. You could also use *premièrement, deuxièmement, troisièmement*. These kinds of words help you to have a structure. For the next section, let us look at two different ways of proceeding, both allowing you to introduce past tenses:

Mais je me souviens d'un voyage qui était moins réussi. Je suis parti avec l'école pour passer une semaine dans les Alpes, et nous avons eu un tas de problèmes. Pour commencer, le bus était peu confortable, et tout le monde se sentait malade pendant le voyage, qui a en plus duré vingt-trois heures. Puis l'hôtel était très sale, et les repas étaient vraiment dégoûtants. Enfin les professeurs se sont fâchés, car quelques élèves ont bu de l'alcool. Mais, j'ai appris une chose importante : je ne repartirai jamais avec l'école.

Again, we have produced a list of reasons with different introductory words, to help learn the presentation. We have also shown we can use the two different past tenses correctly and finished off with a conditional form. We have also given reasons, and used complex sentences with conjunctions, which gives the necessary structures for a good grade. Now let us look at the final part: most of the first two paragraphs used *je*, although we also used the third person. So, we should change this and perhaps use *nous*:

Cette année, je veux partir avec mes parents en France : nous voulons aller dans le Midi, sur la Côte d'Azur. Nous logerons dans un camping, parce que comme ça c'est moins cher. Je sais qu'il y a des désavantages de voyager avec ses parents, mais nous nous entendons bien, et ce sera probablement la dernière fois que nous partirons ensemble, car l'année prochaine, mes copains et moi, on compte aller ensemble en Espagne après notre bac. Là, nous nous amuserons bien !

This final paragraph also has a conclusion, by describing what you are going to do next!

## Hints & tips

Some more things you should do are:

✓ Go to Structures and vocabulary (Chapter 12) for ideas.
✓ Prepare different ways of giving your opinion and work at having alternative options for saying what you think.
✓ Make sure you have a variety of tenses overall.
✓ Have a variety of adjectives and adverbs for opinions — not just bien or difficile. Some of your adjectives should be attached to nouns and be sure to make them agree!
✓ Have a couple of really impressive sentences for your topic area, which you can put in whatever the actual question.
✓ Include at least one conjunction in each paragraph.

## Remember

☞ Giving your opinion and reasons for this opinion is the key to success.
☞ Do not be too obsessive about the word count; you should know on a page of writing how many words you write, so use that as your guide.

Here is an example of a writing code that your teacher might use when marking the first draft of your assignment:

| Code | Meaning |
| --- | --- |
| ∧ | omission/something missing |
| aa | adjectival agreement/problem with agreement of the adjective(s) |
| ap | adjectival position/problem with position of adjective(s) |
| acc | accent missing |
| dict | dictionary/wrong word |
| ew | extra word(s) not required |
| g | gender |
| gr | grammar problem/incorrect grammar |
| np | new paragraph |
| ns | new sentence |
| mv | missing verb |
| mw | missing word |
| punct | punctuation |
| prep | preposition to check |
| rep | repetition |
| s? (text underlined) | not making sense |
| struct | structure – incorrect or does not exist |
| sg/pl | singular/plural |
| sp | spelling |
| t | tense |
| ve | verb ending |
| vt | wrong verb tense |
| wo | word order |
| ww | wrong word |

# Structures and vocabulary

# Introduction

For your Higher French, you will have to produce a variety of pieces of work in French. For Talking, this is both parts of the discussion, and for Writing, the directed writing as well as the writing assignment. You will be assessed in both skills on, amongst other things, your use of structure, your ability to give opinions and reasons and the accurate use of a variety of grammatical structures and vocabulary. The SQA marking scheme mentions the following points relating to Language Resource for a top mark.

## What you should know 👍

★ The language used is detailed and complex.
★ There is good use of adjectives, adverbs, prepositional phrases and, where appropriate, word order.
★ A comprehensive range of verbs/verb forms, tenses and constructions is used.
★ Some modal verbs and infinitives may be used.
★ The candidate is comfortable with the first person of the verb and generally uses a different verb in each sentence.
★ Sentences are mainly complex and accurate.
★ The language flows well.

### Hints & tips ⭐

✓ Practise talking and writing by taking words and phrases from this chapter and making up your own sentences.
✓ Try to make up your own 'complex' sentences, using conjunctions.

# Structure

**Structure** means that your work should be directly related to the topic you are writing or speaking about. You will lose marks for work that is unorganised and irrelevant to the question set.

For the **writing assignment**, structure also means introducing the topic, giving your information and your opinions and coming to a conclusion.

For the **directed writing**, structure means following the bullet points, and addressing each of the points adequately, as well as using some more complex language.

# Giving opinions and reasons

Giving opinions is crucial to any personal response, and also to any presentation or follow-up discussion. It is worth mastering all the vocabulary you learned for National 5, so that it falls easily to you and you don't have to think about it. Make sure you have a variety of phrases, and do not just stick to your favourite three or four. To remind you, here is what you should know already:

| | |
|---|---|
| J'aime, J'adore, Je préfère | *I like, love, prefer* |
| Je n'aime pas, Je déteste | *I don't like, I hate* |
| J'ai horreur de … | *I really hate …* |
| Je trouve que c'est … | *I think that it's …* |
| Je trouve cela formidable | *I find that terrific* |
| Je trouve bête que … | *I find it stupid that …* |
| C'est fantastique, très bien, génial | *It's fantastic, very good, great* |
| intéressant, passionnant, marrant | *interesting, exciting, fun* |
| C'est minable, triste, déprimant | *It's awful, sad, depressing* |
| pénible, nul, ennuyeux | *terrible, no good, boring* |
| Il est mieux/pire de … | *It is better/worse to …* |
| Il y a (Il y avait) trop de … | *There is/are (There was/were) too much/many …* |
| Il n'y a pas assez de … | *There is not enough …* |
| Il serait utile de pouvoir … | *It would be useful to be able to …* |
| À mon avis | *In my opinion* |
| Il faut penser à … | *You have to think about …* |
| Il ne faut pas oublier que … | *We mustn't forget that …* |
| Nous devons …/Nous ne devons pas … | *We should …/We shouldn't …* |
| J'aimerais savoir que … | *I would like to know that …* |
| Je voudrais voir … | *I would like to see …* |

However, for Higher, you need to do more with these. You need to start giving reasons for your opinions. When answering a question in the discussion, on whether you are interested in sport, it is not enough to say:

Non, je n'aime pas le sport.

You have to build on this, and say something like:

Non, je n'aime pas le sport, car je trouve bête qu'on doive sortir quand il pleut pour participer à une activité que je déteste faire.

# Conjunctions

This leads us on to the next part: conjunctions. Get into the habit of giving a reason when you give an opinion, and get into the habit of using conjunctions all the time. It will make your writing or speaking flow better, which means better structured work and a better mark.

## Using conjunctions

Giving reasons for your opinions can be done by simply stating the reason. However, it is much better for your work to use a conjunction, as this allows you to use more complex grammatical structures. How many do you know? Start off with those below, and add more as you come across them, and start using them. Look at these sentences, and try to work out what they mean:

| | | |
|---|---|---|
| mais | but | *J'aime bien le sport, mais je ne suis pas fanatique.* |
| car | because | *J'adore bien ma sœur, car je peux lui parler de tout.* |
| parce que | because | *Je le trouve nul, parce que c'est très difficile et m'embête.* |
| comme | as | *Je ne veux pas sortir, comme il pleut.* |
| donc | so | *Je la trouve minable, donc je préfère ne pas y aller.* |
| par conséquent | therefore | *J'ai trouvé la géo très difficile, par conséquent je n'en fais plus.* |
| quand | when | *Je voulais sortir, quand ma mère m'a persuadé de rester.* |
| lorsque | when | *Lorsque j'étais plus jeune, j'aimais Kylie, mais maintenant, je ne la supporte pas.* |
| pendant que | while | *Pendant que je serai en vacances, je voudrais rester en forme.* |
| comment | how | *Je ne comprends pas comment je peux faire plus d'effort.* |
| si | if | *Je me demande si je l'aime ou non.* |
| ce que | what | *Ce que je n'aime pas, c'est la violence dans la rue.* |

# Grammatical structures

Your grade at Higher (and even your pass/fail) will depend upon your accuracy with grammatical structures. The grammar guide in Appendix 2 will give you an overview of what you should know, but below, briefly, are the main things you should be doing. If you do not understand any of them, then find out what they mean.

## What you should know 👍

- ★ Get the gender and plural form of your nouns right.
- ★ Attach adjectives to nouns with the correct endings and in the correct place.
- ★ Use comparatives.
- ★ Use a variety of negatives with your verbs.
- ★ Use pronouns correctly: that means the correct form, the correct gender and in the correct place.
- ★ Use reflexive pronouns (and reflexive verbs) correctly.
- ★ Use prepositions correctly.

And, of course, knowing about verbs is the single most important thing you can do! You need to get those endings right, which means learning them, but also knowing how to check them in a dictionary, as French has quite a few irregular verbs that do not follow the normal pattern. Here are the tenses you should know and understand: it is your job to match these up with the correct endings.

## The present

The present tense only has one form, unlike in English. Make sure you do not try to translate 'I am working at home' word for word: this is *Je travaille à la maison*. Equally, 'When do you go?' does not need the word *fais* in French.

## The past

You should be able to use at least three tenses in the past. These tenses have various names, although most books refer to them as the perfect, the pluperfect and the imperfect. You should use the perfect to talk about a single event in the past, and the imperfect to describe how things were, used to be, or how things were often:

Je suis parti à six heures du matin.

Il faisait mauvais.

Il faisait souvent mauvais cet hiver.

The pluperfect is used in complex sentences when one thing happened before the other:

*I had already eaten when he arrived.*

J'avais déjà mangé lorsqu'il est arrivé.

You might also come across a verb tense called 'the past historic' or *passé simple*. You do not, however, have to be able to use this for Higher, but some of the texts you read may feature it.

## The future

You should be able to use the informal future, the formal future and the conditional:

On va visiter la France cet été.

J'irai avec mes copines.

J'aimerais aller à Paris.

You should also be able to recognise the subjunctive, and use it at some points in your writing. It may sound difficult, but a French toddler who needs to go to the toilet urgently will shout out *'Il faut que j'aille'*: if a French two-year-old can use the subjunctive, so can you! You will find some examples of this in the chapter on talking (Chapter 9).

# Vocabulary

The vocabulary you will need is the vocabulary you work on as you go through the Course, so make sure you keep a note of it in a way that makes sense to you. That might be in a vocabulary book, in spidergrams or in a folder divided into topics. However, included here are some adjectives and adverbs, as well as some basics that include numbers from earlier for you to revise from, as it will be assumed that you know them. It is amazing how many people get them wrong during the Listening assessments!

## Adjectives

Adjectives are useful for giving opinions, and for improving the quality of your speaking and writing. Here are a few to work from, but add your own as you come across them. If you do not know them, look them up! And remember, if you want the best marks for talking and writing, you should attach these adjectives to nouns. Make sure they are in the correct place – normally after the noun – and that they agree, if necessary:

> C'était une visite affreuse. Ma journée préférée était …

| | | | |
|---|---|---|---|
| affreux | désagréable | nul | rigolo |
| agréable | embêtant | ouvert | sain |
| autoritaire | ennuyeux | parfait | sale |
| barbant | extraordinaire | pas mal | sensible |
| bizarre | gênant | passionnant | seul |
| cher, pas cher | génial | patient | sévère |
| choquant | impressionnant | pénible | strict |
| chouette | magnifique | pratique | sympa |
| cool | malade | préféré | vieux |
| démodé | modeste | raisonnable | |

## Adverbs

Adverbs describe and modify verbs, but they are also very useful with adjectives, to make your language seem more natural:

> C'est absolument nul ! Je le trouve légèrement ennuyeux.

Get into the habit of using them. Here are a few to start with:

| | | | |
|---|---|---|---|
| absolument | extrêmement | même | trop |
| assez | fortement | totalement | un peu |
| bien | jamais | toujours | |
| en général | légèrement | très | |

## Times

| | |
|---|---|
| neuf heures | *nine o'clock* |
| neuf heures et quart | *quarter past nine* |
| neuf heures vingt | *twenty past nine* |
| neuf heures et demie | *half past nine* |
| neuf heures moins le quart | *quarter to nine* |
| neuf heures moins cinq | *five to nine* |
| midi et demi, minuit et demi | *half past tweve* |

*Remember that most official times in French will use the 24-hour clock, and there is no use of a.m. and p.m.*

| | |
|---|---|
| treize heures | *one p.m.* |
| dix-huit heures trente | *6.30 p.m.* |
| le matin | *morning* |
| l'après-midi | *afternoon* |
| le soir | *evening* |
| la nuit | *night* |

## Seasons

| | | | |
|---|---|---|---|
| le printemps | l'été | l'automne | l'hiver |

# Numbers

| | |
|---|---|
| mercredi, le 25 novembre | *Wednesday 25 November* |
| Je suis né le 14 octobre. | *I was born on 14 October.* |
| une semaine | *a week* |
| quinze jours | *a fortnight* |
| un mois | *a month* |
| un an | *a year (used with a number)* |
| J'ai quinze ans. | *I am 15.* |
| une année | *a year (used with an adjective)* |
| une bonne année | *a good year* |
| deux mille treize | *2013* |

*Remember that you should never use measurements like miles when talking and writing in French, but always metres and kilometres.*

Glasgow se trouve à 80 kilomètres d'Edimbourg.

J'habite à 500 mètres de l'école.

*Prices are all in euros and cents: old prices in francs are still in some books, but they will not feature in your exam.*

Un coca coûte 3 euros. J'ai payé 3.50€.

*When writing about yourself, you should use* livre *for 'pounds'.*

Je gagne 20 livres tous les samedis au magasin.

# The weather

| | |
|---|---|
| la météo | *the weather forecast* |
| Quel temps fait-il ? | *What is the weather like?* |
| Il fait beau tous les jours. | *The weather is nice every day.* |
| Il fait du soleil de temps en temps. | *It is sunny now and then.* |
| Il fait chaud. (Il ne fait jamais chaud.) | *It is hot. (It's never hot.)* |
| La température est de 25 degrés. | *It is 25° centigrade.* |
| Il fait mauvais souvent. | *The weather is often bad.* |
| Il fait froid en hiver. | *It is cold in winter.* |
| Il gèle pendant la nuit. | *It freezes over at night.* |
| Il fait du vent assez souvent. | *It is quite often windy.* |
| Il fait du brouillard en automne. | *It is foggy in autumn.* |

⇨

| | |
|---|---|
| Il pleut maintenant. | *It is raining now.* |
| Il neige en hiver. | *It snows in winter.* |
| Il fait de la tempête. | *It is stormy.* |

## Useful words to make your French sound better

| | |
|---|---|
| à mon avis | *to my mind* |
| à peine | *only just, hardly* |
| cependant | *nevertheless, yet* |
| enfin | *finally, well* |
| en outre | *furthermore* |
| il vaut mieux | *it is better to* |
| Je suis très … (Je suis très One Direction.) | *I really like … (I really like One Direction.)* |
| malgré | *despite* |
| même si | *even if* |
| néanmoins | *nevertheless* |
| par ailleurs | *besides* |
| par contre | *however, in contrast* |
| quant à | *as for* |
| sans cesse | *continuously* |
| selon | *according to* |
| surtout | *especially* |
| tandis que | *whereas* |

## Useful verbs to make your French sound better

| | |
|---|---|
| se contenter de | *to make do with* |
| se débrouiller | *to get on, to get by OK* |
| être confronté à | *to be confronted with* |
| être élevé | *to be brought up* |

⇨

| ⇒ | |
|---|---|
| être partagé entre | *to be torn between* |
| être sollicité | *to be in demand* |
| manifester contre | *to protest against* |
| manquer | *to miss* |
| se mettre à | *to get down to, to start* |
| se passer bien | *to go smoothly* |
| profiter de | *to take advantage of* |
| se rappeler | *to remember* |
| réclamer | *to ask for something* |

# Vocabulary for specific topic areas
## Society: family members

| la famille | *family* |
|---|---|
| les parents | *parents* |
| le père | *father* |
| la mère | *mother* |
| le mari | *husband* |
| la femme | *wife* |
| le frère, mon frère aîné/mon frère cadet | *brother, my older/my younger brother* |
| la sœur, ma sœur aînée/ma sœur cadette | *sister, my older/my younger sister* |
| le fils | *son* |
| la fille | *daughter* |
| un jumeau/une jumelle | *twin* |
| le grand-père | *grandfather* |
| la grand-mère | *grandmother* |
| un petit-fils/une petite-fille/les petits-enfants | *grandson/granddaughter/grandchildren* |
| un oncle | *uncle* |
| une tante | *aunt* |
| un cousin/une cousine | *cousin* |
| un neveu | *nephew* |
| une nièce | *niece* |

## Starter sentences

| | |
|---|---|
| Nous sommes quatre dans ma famille. | *There are four of us.* |
| Je n'ai pas de frères/sœurs. | *I don't have any brothers/sisters.* |
| Je suis enfant unique. | *I'm an only child.* |
| J'ai une sœur et deux frères. | *I have a sister and two brothers.* |
| Mon frère/ma sœur s'appelle … | *My brother/sister is called …* |
| Mes parents s'appellent … | *My parents are called …* |
| Mes parents sont séparés/divorcés. | *My parents are separated/divorced.* |
| Je m'entends bien avec mes parents. | *I get on well with my parents.* |
| Mes parents sont très sympa. | *My parents are very nice.* |
| Quelquefois, j'ai des discutes/disputes avec ma mère. | *I sometimes have discussions/arguments with my mum.* |
| Ma sœur est très gentille. | *My sister is very nice.* |
| Je peux discuter de mes problèmes avec … | *I can speak about my problems with …* |
| Je ne m'entends pas bien avec mon frère. | *I don't get on well with my brother.* |
| Mon frère m'énerve. | *My brother annoys me.* |

## Society: family

| | |
|---|---|
| le mariage | *marriage* |
| le divorce | *divorce* |
| le consentement mutuel | *mutual consent* |
| un homme au foyer | *househusband* |
| une femme au foyer | *housewife* |
| un mari/époux | *husband* |
| une épouse/femme | *wife* |
| la cellule familiale | *the family unit* |
| le taux de divorce | *divorce rate* |
| l'éducation des enfants (f) | *raising of the children* |
| l'alliance (f) | *wedding ring* |
| la lune de miel | *honeymoon* |
| la bague des fiançailles | *engagement ring* |
| l'anniversaire de mariage (m) | *wedding anniversary* |
| la grossesse | *pregnancy* |
| l'amitié (m) | *friendship* |

$\Rightarrow$

| | |
|---|---|
| la relation | *relationship* |
| les fiançailles (f) | *engagement* |
| les beaux-parents (m) | *in-laws* |
| un casse-tête | *major problem, a headache* |
| grandir | *to grow up* |
| le planning familial | *family planning* |
| le comportement | *behaviour* |
| le foyer | *the home* |
| le concubinage | *living together* |
| la cohabitation | *living together* |
| le congé maternité | *maternity leave* |
| l'état civil (m) | *marital status* |
| le mariage civil | *registry marriage* |
| le PACS | *contract between two people living together, civil partnership* |
| la famille (monoparentale) | *(single-parent) family* |
| l'union libre (f) | *living together* |
| le conflit des générations | *the generation gap* |

## Society: impact of the digital age

| | |
|---|---|
| connecté | *logged on* |
| le cyber commerce | *e-commerce* |
| l'écran (m) | *screen* |
| le fichier | *file* |
| un informaticien | *IT technician* |
| l'internaute (m/f) | *internet user* |
| le mail | *email message* |
| le moteur de recherche | *search engine* |
| la pièce jointe | *attachment* |
| le pirate | *hacker* |
| le réseau | *network* |
| le site Web | *website* |
| le site Web de réseau social | *social networking site* |

⇨

| | |
|---|---|
| le SMS | *text message* |
| les solutions informatiques (f) | *IT solutions* |
| le soutien | *support* |
| TIC : Techniques de l'Information et de la Communication (f) | *ICT: Information and Communication Technologies* |
| le virus | *computer virus* |

⇨

## Society problems: drugs/alcohol/smoking

| | |
|---|---|
| le tabagisme | *addiction to smoking* |
| le tabagisme passif | *passive smoking* |
| le SIDA | *AIDS* |
| le préservatif | *condom* |
| le toxicomane | *drug addict* |
| le trafiquant | *drug dealer* |
| le cancer du poumon | *lung cancer* |
| le centre de réadaption | *rehabilitation centre* |
| le cerveau | *brain* |
| la cirrhose du foie | *cirrhosis of the liver* |
| la conduite en état d'ivresse | *drink-driving* |
| les dommages irréversibles (m) | *irreversible damage* |
| les drogues dures (f) | *hard drugs* |
| les drogues douces (f) | *soft drugs* |
| le foie | *liver* |
| la guérison | *cure* |
| la gueule de bois | *hangover* |
| l'héroïnomane (m/f) | *heroin addict* |
| l'interdiction (f) | *ban* |
| l'ivresse (f) | *drunkenness* |
| le manque | *withdrawal symptoms* |
| la poussée de stupéfiants | *drug-pushing* |
| les problèmes respiratoires (m) | *breathing problems* |
| les retombées (f) | *side-effects* |
| le sevrage | *weaning off drugs* |

⇨

| | |
|---|---|
| ⇨ | |
| le stupéfiant | *drug* |
| la toxicomanie (f) | *drug addiction* |
| la toux du fumeur | *smoker's cough* |
| la volonté | *will power* |
| avoir/former une dépendance à | *to be/become addicted to* |
| boire à l'excès | *to drink to excess* |
| se droguer | *to take drugs* |
| empêcher | *to prevent* |
| fumer | *to smoke* |
| nuire à | *to harm* |

## Learning: school subjects

| | |
|---|---|
| l'allemand (m) | *German* |
| l'anglais (m) | *English* |
| la biologie | *biology* |
| la chimie | *chemistry* |
| le commerce | *business management* |
| le dessin | *art* |
| l'EMT (f) | *craft and design* |
| l'EPS (f) | *PE* |
| l'espagnol (m) | *Spanish* |
| le français | *French* |
| la géographie | *geography* |
| l'histoire (f) | *history* |
| l'informatique (f) | *IT* |
| les maths (m) | *maths* |
| la musique | *music* |
| la politique/l'instruction civique (f) | *modern studies* |
| la physique | *physics* |
| les sciences nat (f) | *science* |
| le sport | *sport* |
| la technologie | *technological studies* |

## School (general)

| | |
|---|---|
| le collège/CES | *secondary school (S1–4)* |
| le lycée | *secondary school (S5/6)* |
| le bac/baccalauréat | *equivalent to Highers* |
| la bibliothèque | *library* |
| le bulletin | *report* |
| la cantine | *canteen* |
| le cours | *lesson* |
| les devoirs (m) | *homework* |
| l'élève (m/f) | *pupil* |
| les études (f) | *study, schoolwork* |
| l'examen (m) | *exam* |
| la fac/l'université (f) | *uni/university* |
| le laboratoire | *laboratory* |
| la matière | *subject* |
| la pause de midi | *lunchtime* |
| le/la professeur | *teacher* |
| la récréation/récré | *morning interval, break* |
| la salle de classe | *classroom* |
| les vacances (f) | *holidays* |
| les grandes vacances (f) | *summer holidays* |
| les vacances de Pâques, de Noël (f) | *Easter, Christmas holidays* |

*Remember that French students would refer to fifth year as* seconde *and use* terminale *for the last year in school. The equivalent of Highers would be the* bac.

## Starter sentences

| | |
|---|---|
| Je vais passer mes examens en mai. | *I'm going to sit my exams in May.* |
| J'espère réussir à mes examens. | *I hope to pass my exams.* |
| J'ai reçu de bonnes notes en … | *I got good marks in …* |
| Ma matière préférée est le français. | *My favourite subject is French.* |
| Ce que je n'aime pas du tout, c'est … | *What I really don't like is …* |
| Je pense que le prof est moche. | *I think that the teacher is awful.* |

⇨

| | |
|---|---|
| Je trouve que j'ai trop de devoirs. | *I have too much homework, I think.* |
| L'année prochaine, je vais continuer mes études au lycée. | *I'm staying on next year.* |

## Learning

| | |
|---|---|
| apprendre | *to learn* |
| le centre d'information et d'orientation | *careers advisory centre* |
| la classe | *class* |
| le concours | *competitive exam* |
| le conseiller d'orientation | *careers adviser* |
| le contrôle | *test, assessment* |
| l'école des beaux-arts (f) | *Art College, often simply referred to as* les beaux-arts |
| enseigner | *to teach* |
| les épreuves, une épreuve | *the individual parts (written, oral, practical, etc.) that make up any given examination* |
| la note | *mark* |
| le programme, le programme scolaire | *curriculum* |
| le taux de réussite | *success rate* |
| le/la titulaire | *holder (of a qualification)* |

## Employability: jobs and professions

*Remember when talking about what a person does, you do not need* un/le: mon père est dentiste.

| | |
|---|---|
| acteur/actrice | *actor/actress* |
| agent de police | *policeman/woman* |
| agriculteur | *farmer* |
| avocat | *lawyer* |
| boucher/bouchère | *butcher* |
| boulanger/boulangère | *baker* |
| caissier/caissière | *cashier* |
| chauffeur de taxi | *taxi driver* |
| chômeur/chômeuse | *unemployed person* |

⇨

| | |
|---|---|
| coiffeur/coiffeuse | *hairdresser* |
| cuisinier/cuisinière | *cook* |
| dentiste | *dentist* |
| directeur/directrice | *headteacher or director* |
| éléctricien/éléctricienne | *electrician* |
| facteur/factrice | *postie* |
| hôtesse de l'air | *air stewardess* |
| infirmier/infirmière | *nurse* |
| ingénieur | *engineer* |
| jardinier/jardinière | *gardener* |
| journaliste | *journalist* |
| maçon | *bricklayer, builder* |
| mécanicien/mécanicienne | *mechanic* |
| médecin | *doctor* |
| patron/patronne | *boss or owner* |
| PDG | *managing director* |
| plombier/plombière | *plumber* |
| professeur | *teacher* |
| secrétaire | *secretary* |
| serveur/serveuse | *waiter/waitress, barman, shop assistant* |
| technicien/technicienne | *technician* |
| vendeur/vendeuse | *shop/sales assistant* |

## Starter sentences

| | |
|---|---|
| Ma mère est professeur. | *My mum is a teacher.* |
| Je voudrais devenir infirmière. | *I'd like to be a nurse.* |
| Je vais aller en fac. | *I'm going to go to university.* |
| Je veux continuer mes études. | *I intend to stay on at school.* |
| Le samedi, je travaille dans un café. | *I work in a café on Saturdays.* |
| J'ai un petit boulot comme vendeuse. | *I have a part-time job in a shop.* |

## Employability, general

| | |
|---|---|
| l'artisanat (m) | *Arts and Crafts* |
| le chef d'entreprise | *company manager* |
| l'expatrié (m) | *expat* |
| gérer | *to manage* |
| l'intérim, intérimaire (m/f) | *temp, temporary worker* |
| le métier | *profession* |
| le monde de l'entreprise | *the business world* |

## Culture, travel: methods of transport

| | |
|---|---|
| en auto/voiture | *by car* |
| en autobus/car | *by bus* |
| en avion | *by plane* |
| en bateau | *by boat* |
| en métro | *by underground* |
| à moto | *by motorbike* |
| à pied | *on foot* |
| en train | *by train* |
| à vélo | *by bike* |

## Starter sentences

| | |
|---|---|
| Je vais au collège à pied, normalement. | *Usually I walk to school.* |
| Nous sommes allés en bus. | *We went by bus.* |
| Quand il pleut, je prends le bus. | *I go by bus when it's raining.* |
| Je préfère aller en voiture, c'est plus vite. | *I prefer going by car, it's quicker.* |
| Nous sommes allés en France en train. | *We went to France by train.* |
| Je préfère aller à vélo, c'est plus facile. | *I prefer to go by bike, it's easier.* |

## Culture: travel

| | |
|---|---|
| l'auberge de jeunesse (f) | *youth hostel* |
| le bord de la mer | *seaside* |
| le centre touristique | *tourist resort* |
| le circuit touristique | *tourist circuit* |
| la colonie (le club) de vacances | *holiday camp* |
| le coût de la vie | *cost of living* |
| la croisière | *cruise* |
| le dépaysement | *change of scenery* |
| la détente | *relaxation* |
| les distractions (f) | *things to do* |
| l'emploi saisonnier (m) | *seasonal job* |
| l'estivant (m) | *holiday maker* |
| l'évasion (f) | *escape* |
| la haute saison | *high season* |
| l'hébergement (m) | *accommodation* |
| le littoral | *seashore* |
| la pension | *guest house* |
| la résidence secondaire | *holiday home* |
| le retour à la nature | *return to nature* |
| la station balnéaire | *seaside resort* |
| le tourisme | *tourism* |
| le tourisme rural | *cottage holidays* |
| le vacancier | *holiday maker* |
| la vie nocturne | *night life* |
| les vacances en location (f) | *self-catering holidays* |
| le voyage | *trip* |
| partir en vacances | *to go on holiday* |
| se détendre | *to relax* |
| abîmer | *to spoil* |
| apporter | *to bring* |
| approfondir votre connaissance du monde | *to deepen one's knowledge of the world* |
| élargir ses horizons | *to broaden one's horizons* |
| ouvrir l'esprit | *to open the mind* |

# Culture: media

| | |
|---|---|
| à la une | *on the front page* |
| la bande dessinée, BD | *comic, also often a graphic novel* |
| le courrier du cœur | *agony aunt column* |
| la critique | *review* |
| le dessin animé | *cartoon* |
| la diffusion | *broadcast* |
| le divertissement | *entertainment* |
| le dossier | *issue, area of concern* |
| l'éditeur (m) | *publisher* |
| l'émission (f) | *programme* |
| l'émission d'actualité (f) | *news programme* |
| l'exemplaire (m) | *copy* |
| les faits divers (m) | *news in brief* |
| le feuilleton | *TV series, soap* |
| les gros titres (m) | *headlines* |
| les hebdomadaires (m) | *weekly newspapers* |
| les infos (f) | *news* |
| le journal | *newspaper* |
| le journaliste | *journalist* |
| la libre parole | *free speech* |
| la liberté de la presse | *freedom of the press* |
| le magasin de journaux | *newsagent's* |
| le magazine d'information | *news programme* |
| les médias (m) | *media* |
| les petites annonces (f) | *classified ads* |
| la presse de sensation | *tabloid press* |
| la publicité | *advertising* |
| la question d'actualité | *topical issue* |
| le quotidien | *a daily* |
| le quotidien populaire/un tabloïde | *tabloid* |
| le rédacteur | *editor* |

⇨

⇨

| | |
|---|---|
| le reportage sportif | *sports programme* |
| la revue d'actualité | *news magazine* |
| la rubrique (sportive) | *(sports) section/column* |
| les ventes (f) | *sales* |
| la vie privée | *private life* |

## Contexts and topics of Higher French

| Society | Family and friends | Becoming an adult/new family structure/marriage/partnership/gang culture/bullying/social influences and pressures |
|---|---|---|
| | Lifestyle | Teenage problems, e.g. smoking, drugs, alcohol |
| | Media | Impact of the digital age |
| | Global languages | Minority languages and their importance/association with culture |
| | Citizenship | Global citizenship/democracy/politics/power |
| Learning | Learning in context | Understanding self as a learner, e.g. learning styles/importance of language learning |
| | Education | Advantages/disadvantages of higher or further education, choosing a university/college, lifelong learning |
| Employability | Jobs | Getting a summer job, planning for future jobs/higher education, gap year, career path, equality in the workplace |
| | Work and CVs | Preparing for a job interview/importance of language in global contexts, job opportunities |
| Culture | Planning a trip | Taking a gap year/working abroad (mobility)/travel |
| | Other countries | Living in a multicultural society/stereotypes/ prejudice and racism |
| | Celebrating a special event | Social influences on/importance of traditions, customs and beliefs in another country |
| | Literature of another country | Literature – analysis and evaluation |
| | Film and television | Studying the media of another country |

# Appendix 2

## Grammar guide: talking and writing

| Grammar | Judging evidence at Higher<br>The candidate: |
|---|---|
| Word order | • has control of different linguistic conventions in straightforward expressions and most more complex structures, e.g. noun/adjective order, relative and subordinate clauses<br>• shows awareness of different linguistic conventions, e.g. noun/adjective order |
| Person | • uses subject and object pronouns consistently and shows awareness of the use of indirect object pronouns<br>• uses reflexive and relative pronouns with common verbs in appropriate tenses |
| Tense and mood | • uses a range of tenses as appropriate, in particular present, future, perfect, imperfect, pluperfect, conditional<br>• can ask a range of questions in different ways and can articulate commands<br>• can use modal verbs plus infinitive in a range of tenses as appropriate<br>• can use less common irregular verbs |
| Articles | • uses articles/determiners consistently and accurately |
| Cases and agreement | • shows some control of cases as appropriate in the language<br>• uses correct adjective agreements with wide range of nouns (regular and irregular)<br>• can use less common comparatives and superlatives |
| Prepositions | • can use common and less common prepositions and shows awareness of prepositional effects |
| Gender | • shows awareness of noun genders<br>• uses correct adjective agreement with a wider range of nouns (regular and some irregular forms) |

# Appendix 3

## Marking instructions for talking

| Content | Accuracy | Language resource | Pegged marks |
|---|---|---|---|
| The candidate: | | | |
| • uses content which is comprehensive, relevant and well organised<br>• expresses a wide range of ideas and opinions<br>• readily goes beyond minimum responses<br>• readily adapts learned material as appropriate to the discussion<br>• deals confidently with unpredictable elements<br>• shows little, if any, undue hesitation<br>• readily takes the initiative<br>• covers at least two contexts | • demonstrates a very good degree of grammatical accuracy corresponding to the level<br>• may make a few errors which do not detract from the overall impression<br>• uses pronunciation and intonation which are sufficient to be readily understood by a speaker of the language | • immediately understands almost all of what is said<br>• uses a wide range of **detailed and complex** language<br>• uses a wide range of structures<br>• uses a wide range of verbs/verb forms, tenses and other language features<br>• may use some idiomatic language and expressions<br>• may use some interjections and/or connectives<br>• may occasionally seek clarification in the modern language | 30 or 27 |
| • uses content which is mostly relevant and well organised<br>• expresses a range of ideas and opinions<br>• goes beyond minimum responses<br>• uses learned material but not always appropriately<br>• deals with unpredictable elements<br>• may hesitate occasionally but recovers successfully<br>• occasionally takes the initiative<br>• covers at least two contexts | • demonstrates a good degree of grammatical accuracy corresponding to the level<br>• may make errors which occasionally detract from the overall impression<br>• uses pronunciation and intonation which can mostly be understood by a speaker of the language | • understands almost all of what is said<br>• uses a range of **detailed and complex** language<br>• uses a range of structures<br>• uses a range of verbs/verb forms, tenses and other language features<br>• may attempt to use some idiomatic language and expressions<br>• may attempt to use some interjections and/or connectives<br>• may seek clarification in the modern language | 24 or 21 |

| Content | Accuracy | Language resource | Pegged marks |
|---|---|---|---|
| <ul><li>uses content which is generally relevant and well organised</li><li>expresses some ideas and opinions</li><li>attempts to go beyond minimum responses</li><li>mostly deals with unpredictable elements</li><li>may rely on the use of learned material</li><li>may hesitate occasionally, thereby affecting the flow of the discussion</li><li>may attempt to take the initiative but not always successfully</li><li>may not cover at least two contexts</li></ul> | <ul><li>demonstrates an adequate degree of grammatical accuracy corresponding to the level</li><li>makes errors which detract from the overall impression</li><li>uses pronunciation and intonation which are sufficient to be understood by a speaker of the language, although some points may not be immediately clear</li></ul> | <ul><li>understands most of what is said</li><li>attempts to use a range of **detailed and complex** language</li><li>attempts to use a range of structures</li><li>uses a few different verbs/verb forms, tenses and other language features</li><li>uses language which is perhaps repetitive</li><li>may require occasional prompting and/or repetition</li><li>may attempt to use some interjections and/or connectives but not always successfully</li><li>may attempt to seek clarification in the modern language</li></ul> | 18 or 15 |
| <ul><li>uses content which at times may not be relevant and well organised</li><li>expresses limited ideas and opinions</li><li>tends not to go beyond minimum responses</li><li>has difficulty dealing with some unpredictable elements</li><li>relies heavily on the use of learned material</li><li>hesitates in many responses, thereby affecting the flow of the discussion</li><li>rarely takes the initiative</li><li>may not cover at least two contexts</li></ul> | <ul><li>demonstrates an inadequate degree of grammatical accuracy corresponding to the level</li><li>makes errors which often impede communication</li><li>uses pronunciation and intonation which are generally sufficient to be understood by a speaker of the language, although some points may not be immediately clear</li></ul> | <ul><li>may have difficulty in understanding much of what is said</li><li>uses a limited amount of **detailed and complex** language</li><li>uses a limited range of structures</li><li>uses a limited amount of verbs/verb forms, tenses and other language features</li><li>requires some prompting and/or repetition</li><li>frequently uses language which is not appropriate to the level</li><li>may seek clarification in the modern language but often unsuccessfully</li></ul> | 12 or 9 |
| <ul><li>uses content which is basic, irrelevant and disorganised</li><li>expresses ideas and opinions with difficulty</li><li>is unable to go beyond the use of learned material</li><li>has difficulty dealing with most unpredictable elements</li><li>hesitates throughout, thereby seriously affecting the flow of the discussion</li><li>does not take the initiative</li><li>may not cover at least two contexts</li></ul> | <ul><li>demonstrates serious grammatical inaccuracy corresponding to the level</li><li>makes errors which impede communication throughout</li><li>uses pronunciation and intonation which are often insufficient to be understood by a speaker of the language, and many points may not be clear</li></ul> | <ul><li>may have difficulty in understanding most of what is said</li><li>uses a very limited amount of **detailed and complex** language</li><li>uses a very limited range of structures</li><li>uses a very limited amount of verbs/verb forms, tenses and other language features</li><li>requires frequent prompting and/or repetition</li><li>mostly uses language which is not appropriate to the level</li><li>may demonstrate other language interference</li><li>may not seek clarification in the modern language</li></ul> | 6 or 3 |

| Content | Accuracy | Language resource | Pegged marks |
|---|---|---|---|
| • uses content which is basic, irrelevant and disorganised <br> • expresses no ideas and opinions <br> • is unable to deal with unpredictable elements <br> • hesitates throughout, thereby seriously impeding communication <br> • is unable to take the initiative <br> • may not cover at least two contexts | • uses language which is almost completely inaccurate <br> • makes errors which seriously impede communication throughout <br> • uses pronunciation and intonation which are insufficient to be understood by a speaker of the language | • is unable to understand much of what is said <br> • uses no **detailed and complex** language <br> • uses very few, if any, structures <br> • uses very few, if any, verbs/verb forms, tenses and other language features <br> • requires constant prompting and/or repetition <br> • uses language which is not appropriate to the level <br> • may demonstrate several examples of other language interference <br> • is unable to seek clarification in the modern language | 0 |

# Appendix 4

## Marking instructions for directed writing

For the directed writing, you are expected to address **all six** bullet points, including **both** parts of the first bullet point.

i) If you fail to address one of the bullet points, the maximum mark that can be awarded is 16.

ii) If you fail to address two of the bullet points, the maximum mark that can be awarded is 12.

iii) If you fail to address three or more of the bullet points, the maximum mark that can be awarded is 0.

| Mark | Content | Accuracy | Language resource |
|---|---|---|---|
| 20 | ● The content is comprehensive.<br>● The candidate addresses all bullet points fully and may also provide additional relevant information<br>● The language flows well. | ● The language is accurate throughout. However, where the candidate attempts to go beyond the range of the task, a slightly higher number of inaccuracies need not detract from the overall impression.<br>● The candidate uses a comprehensive range of verbs accurately, and tenses are consistent and accurate.<br>● The candidate demonstrates confident handling of all aspects of grammar and accuracy in spelling, and, where appropriate, word order. The language may contain a number of minor errors, or even one serious error. | ● The candidate uses detailed and complex language throughout.<br>● There is a wide range of adjectives, adverbs and prepositional phrases.<br>● They use a comprehensive range of verbs/verb forms, tenses and constructions. |
| 16 | ● The content is clear.<br>● The candidate addresses bullet points clearly, although one bullet point may not be addressed.<br>● Generally the language flows well. | ● The language is mostly accurate. Where the candidate attempts to use detailed and complex language, errors may detract from the overall impression.<br>● The candidate uses a range of verbs accurately, and tenses are generally consistent and accurate.<br>● There may be a few errors in spelling, adjective endings and, where relevant, word order and case endings.<br>● Use of accents, where relevant, is not always secure. | ● The candidate uses language which is mostly detailed and complex.<br>● In one bullet point the language may be less detailed and complex than might otherwise be expected at this level.<br>● The candidate uses a range of verbs/verb forms and other constructions.<br>● Overall the writing is competent but there may be some repetition of structures. |

| Mark | Content | Accuracy | Language resource |
|---|---|---|---|
| 12 | • The content is adequate.<br>• The candidate addresses bullet points adequately, however two of the bullet points may not be addressed. | • The language may be accurate in most of the bullet points. However, in the others, control of the language may deteriorate significantly.<br>• Verbs are generally correct.<br>• The candidate may use tenses inconsistently, with present tenses used at times instead of past tenses.<br>• There may be errors in spelling, adjective endings and other parts of speech, as well as in word order, cases and the use of accents (where relevant).<br>• Overall, there is more correct than incorrect. | • The candidate gives some examples of detailed and complex language.<br>• The candidate attempts to use a range of vocabulary and structures, although the language may be repetitive.<br>• The candidate attempts to use a range of verbs and tenses.<br>• Sentences may be brief. |
| 8 | • The content may be limited.<br>• The writing may be presented as a single paragraph. | • The language is inaccurate and after the first bullet point the control of the language may deteriorate significantly.<br>• Verbs are generally incorrect and the candidate has difficulty in using different tenses.<br>• There are errors, which may be serious, in spelling, adjectival endings and many other parts of speech, as well as in word order, cases and accents (where relevant).<br>• Some points may not be immediately understood by a speaker of the language. | • The candidate demonstrates a limited use of detailed and complex language.<br>• The language is repetitive, with a limited range of vocabulary and structures.<br>• Sentences are brief.<br>• There may be other language interference and/or an example of serious dictionary misuse. |
| 4 | • The content is limited.<br>• The candidate has difficulty in addressing the bullet points. | • The language is inaccurate throughout and there is little control of language.<br>• Most of the verbs are incorrect and the candidate has great difficulty in using tenses.<br>• There are many serious errors in spelling, adjectival endings and many other parts of speech, as well as in word order, cases and accents (where relevant).<br>• Several points may not be understood by a speaker of the language. | • The candidate uses little, if any, detailed and complex language.<br>• There is a very limited range of verbs, vocabulary and structures.<br>• Sentences are very brief.<br>• There may be several examples of other language interference and/or serious dictionary misuse. |

121

# Marking instructions for Assignment-writing

| Content | Accuracy | Language resource | Pegged marks |
|---|---|---|---|
| The candidate: | | | |
| • addresses the title in a full and balanced way<br>• uses content which is relevant<br>• expresses a wide range of ideas, opinions and reasons<br>• presents different arguments or viewpoints and draws a conclusion<br>• writes in a very structured and organised way and the language flows well | • demonstrates a very good degree of grammatical accuracy corresponding to the level, although may make a few errors which do not detract from the overall impression<br>• demonstrates a very good degree of accuracy in spelling and, where appropriate, word order | • uses **detailed and complex** language throughout<br>• uses a wide range of structures<br>• uses a wide range of verbs/verb forms, tenses (if appropriate) and other language features | 20 |
| • addresses the title competently<br>• uses content which is mostly relevant<br>• expresses a range of ideas, opinions and reasons<br>• presents different arguments or viewpoints and draws a conclusion<br>• writes in a structured and organised way | • demonstrates a good degree of grammatical accuracy corresponding to the level. Errors may occasionally detract from the overall impression<br>• demonstrates a good degree of accuracy in spelling and, where appropriate, word order | • mostly uses **detailed and complex** language<br>• uses a range of structures<br>• uses a range of verbs/verb forms, tenses (if appropriate) and other language features<br>• may occasionally repeat structures, verbs, etc | 16 |
| • addresses the title fairly competently<br>• uses content which is generally relevant<br>• expresses some ideas, opinions and reasons<br>• attempts to present different arguments or viewpoints and to draw a conclusion<br>• writes with an adequate sense of structure and writing is mostly organised | • demonstrates an adequate degree of grammatical accuracy corresponding to the level, although errors, which occasionally may be serious, detract from the overall impression<br>• demonstrates an adequate degree of accuracy in spelling and, where appropriate, word order<br>• produces more correct language than incorrect | • attempts to use **detailed and complex** language<br>• attempts to use a range of structures<br>• uses a few different verbs/verb forms, tenses (if appropriate) and other language features<br>• may use fairly repetitive language<br>• may use some lists | 12 |
| • uses content which at times may not be relevant to the title<br>• expresses limited ideas, opinions and reasons<br>• may find it difficult to present different arguments or viewpoints and to draw a conclusion<br>• writes with a limited sense of structure and writing may not be well organised | • demonstrates an inadequate degree of grammatical accuracy corresponding to the level<br>• makes errors, many of which are serious and impede communication<br>• demonstrates an inadequate degree of accuracy in spelling and, where appropriate, word order<br>• may demonstrate evidence of misuse of the dictionary<br>• may include other language interference | • uses a limited amount of **detailed and complex** language<br>• uses a limited range of structures<br>• uses a limited amount of verbs/verb forms, and other language features<br>• uses language which is largely repetitive<br>• demonstrates an over-reliance on the use of lists | 8 |

| Content | Accuracy | Language resource | Pegged marks |
|---|---|---|---|
| • uses content which may have little relevance to the title<br>• expresses very limited ideas, opinions and reasons<br>• presents few arguments or viewpoints and has difficulty drawing a conclusion<br>• demonstrates little sense of structure or organisation | • demonstrates serious grammatical inaccuracies corresponding to the level<br>• makes serious errors which impede communication throughout<br>• demonstrates an insufficient degree of accuracy in spelling and, where appropriate, word order<br>• demonstrates evidence of misuse of the dictionary<br>• may include other language interference | • uses a very limited amount of **detailed and complex** language<br>• uses a very limited range of structures<br>• uses a very limited amount of verbs/verb forms, and other language features<br>• uses repetitive language | 4 |
| • uses content which is irrelevant to the title<br>• does not express any ideas, opinions or reasons<br>• is unable to present any arguments or viewpoints and/or draw a conclusion<br>• is unable to write with any structure or organisation | • demonstrates little or no evidence of grammatical accuracy corresponding to the level<br>• has great difficulty in spelling most words correctly<br>• demonstrates little or no knowledge of word order<br>• frequently demonstrates evidence of misuse of the dictionary<br>• includes frequent other language interference | • does not use **detailed and complex** language<br>• makes little or no use of structures, verbs/verb forms and other language features | 0 |

# Space for extra vocabulary and notes